25 Uncle Sam Patterns FOR CARVERS

Al Streetman

with a foreword by Harold Enlow

Schiffer Publishing Ltd

77 Lower Valley Road, Atglen, PA 19310

Dedication

This one is for Lori and Lance.
A great daughter, and a super son-in-law.
I couldn't ask for a better family.

Acknowledgments

The following people helped make this book possible. I thank you all.

Jack Lisiecki: As always, your photography was great.

Marilynn Jones: Without your help and assistance, my book would still be trapped somewhere on the computer disk.

Delta Technical Coatings, Inc.: The paint samples for Uncle Sam were excellent, and satisfactory in all respects.

Wood Carvers Supply, Inc., Englewood, Florida: For high quality carving tools and supplies

Published by Schiffer Publishing, Ltd.
77 Lower Valley Road
Atglen, PA 19310
Please write for a free catalog.
This book may be purchased from the publisher.
Please include $2.95 postage.
Try your bookstore first.

We are interested in hearing from authors
with book ideas on related subjects.

Library of Congress Cataloging-in-Publication Data
25 Uncle Sam patterns for carvers/Al Streetman: with a foreword by Harold Enlow.
p. cm.–(A Schiffer book for woodcarvers)
ISBN 0-88740-717-X
1. Wood-carving–patterns. 2. Wood-carved figurines. 3. Uncle Sam (Nickname) in art. I. Title. II. Title: Twenty-five Uncle Sam patterns for carvers. III. Series.
TT199.7.S77 1995
731.4'62–dc20 94-23250
CIP

Printed in China.
ISBN: 0-88740-717-X

Contents

FOREWORD

When I think of Uncle Sam, I think of a wholesome, all-American patriot who is a mixture of all that is good in our country. The "Uncle" figure is one that most of us regard as a protector and role model, so we see him as one of the good guys. Uncle Sam lends himself well to small statues, and is a great idea for a carving book. Since I was just a kid, I've seen him portrayed in many ways. I've seen him sculpted, painted, made into ceramic molds, as banks, and used a great deal in my part of the country as a mailbox stand. I've carved him a few times over the years. The one that jumps first into my mind is the one that I made with President Jimmy Carter's face. I still save pictures and clippings for future reference in case the urge strikes me to carve him again.

Al Streetman has collected together some of his ideas, and made them into usable patterns which should get you off to a quick start on carving this ever popular home-grown character. If you are a flag-waving, red-blooded American, or even if you just like firecrackers, you'll want to carve all the patterns in this book. Al has done a fine job in writing this little volume. It is easily understood, as an instruction book should be. It shouldn't be long before you are busily designing your own ideas and making the chips fly.

Al, I wish you great success with your publication of *25 Uncle Sam Patterns for Carvers*. I'll be patiently waiting for my autographed copy.

Harold L. Enlow,
November, 1993.
Dogpatch, Arkansas

Introduction

Uncle Sam is a colorful character, and a favorite with decorators and collectors of items having an Americana theme. He is fun to carve and paint, and when put on display, will brighten up any room he is in. He is also one of my best, and most steady, sellers. I wrote this book to provide beginning wood carvers with a project which they could accomplish with a minimum of tools and frustration, and also to provide intermediate and advanced wood carvers with an assortment of Uncle Sams in different poses. I have not devoted any chapters to the selection, sharpening, or use of woodcarving tools. There are already an abundance of books about this on the market. Except for the actual carving project, I have not included specific carving instructions. I have found that each carver has his or her own style, and each has their preference for which tool to use in a particular area, or to achieve a particular effect.

The patterns in this book include approximate dimensions of the side and front views, as an aid in selecting the properly sizes of wood. If you desire a larger or smaller version, simply enlarge or shrink the pattern on a photocopying machine. You may also want to use the photocopying machine to make several sizes of the hand template. This way you will be sure to have a hand outline that is the proper size for the Uncle Sam you carve.

I use Basswood whenever possible, but any soft wood such as Jelutong, clear Spruce, or Sugar/White Pine will work equally well. If possible, use a bandsaw with a 1/8" blade to cut out the side profile. On the patterns with extended arms, you may wish to cut out the front profile instead. Experienced carvers may wish to saw out both the front and side profiles where feasible. The bandsaw will allow you to release the rough version of Uncle Sam from the block of wood faster than trying to use a coping saw or other means to cut out the pattern. As I mentioned in my previous book, if you don't have a bandsaw, now is the time to become real good friends with someone who does have one!

General Notes

1. Trace the pattern, or make a copy of it on a photocopying machine. Glue the pattern you copied or traced onto some heavy paper such as poster paper or a manila file folder. When the glue is dry, cut out the pattern. This method will prevent you from ruining the master patterns in your book. Also, make a copy of the hand template, glue it to some heavy paper, and cut it out. We will use it at a later step in the carving project, when it is time to make the hands and fit them to the body.

2. Lay your pattern on the wood , trace the outline of it, and saw it out. Remember my note about the patterns with extended arms.

3. You should now have a rough blank ready to be carved.

4. Use your own techniques and style to bring the carving to the finished stage.

5. You will notice that some of the patterns do not show hands on the bodies. This method allows you to carve the body, then decide on the size and style of hand you want to use for that carving. (This is where you will put the hand template to work). Many times the type of hand will be determined by what accessories you are going to include with the carving (skyrocket, firecrackers, etc.). Because you are carving the hand separately from the body, you can orient it to take advantage of the wood grain when you saw it out.

6. We are also going to carve the head separately from the main body. This gives you several advantages: (1) if you make a mistake on the head or body, the other part won't be ruined ; (2) you can assemble the head to the body looking straight ahead, or you can turn it to one side (turning the head to one side will give more "life" to your carvings); (3) You can "mix and match" different heads with different bodies, therefore gaining more variations from a given number of patterns. After the head and body are carved, the neck will be adjusted for the proper length.

On the patterns where the head is to be carved separately, I have put dotted lines inside the body pattern to give you an idea where to drill the neck hole. Also, if there is no head pattern shown separately on the pattern page, this indicates that this project is better carved from one solid piece (such as the Weathervane, Roly-Polies, etc.).

Tips

1. I often use various sizes of plastic-head quilting pins to make eyes. Mark where you want the eyes to be on the finished carving. Using a drill and bit that is slightly larger than the pin head you are going to use, make a hole for each eye.

Using wire cutters, snip off the pin head, leaving about 1/4" of the pin attached to the head.

Insert the pin head into the eye socket, with the pin end going in first. Use a nail set to seat the head into the hole until only a small orb protrudes. This gives a fairly realistic eye without too much effort on your part. For extra detail, remove a triangular shaped piece of wood from the sides of the pin head. This will make a very realistic eye when it is painted.

2. When buying wood, whether it be Basswood, Spruce, or some other type, try to pick the **lightest** pieces. They tend to have less fat and sap in them, so they are **easier** to carve.

3. An easy way to make stars is to take a stylus or toothpick and put a dot of white paint where you want the star to be. Starting inside the dot, while the paint is still wet, drag the tip of the stylus or toothpick toward the edge and out to make a line. Do this for all five points of the star. The bigger you make the dot of paint to begin with, and the further you drag each line outside of the dot, the bigger the star will be.

4. I normally use the same thickness of wood for the head as I use for the body. This provides plenty of wood for a big, floppy hat and brim.

General Painting Suggestions

I have included suggested colors for all patterns. If you have a preference for a different color scheme, by all means use it. After all, it's your Uncle Sam. You may want to paint white stars on a blue coat, or use a different vest color. There is no "official" paint scheme for Uncle Sam, so have fun carving and painting him.

Listed below are the colors produced by Delta Technical Coatings, Inc. which I have found to be suitable for painting Uncle Sam. I have used these colors, and the results were excellent. I hope this will help minimize your confusion when trying to sort through the maze of paint brands and colors at your hobby or craft store.

Fleshtone
Sweetheart Blush
White
Blue Heaven
Navy Blue
Black
Napthol Red
Antique Gold
Pearl
Dark Forest Green
Boston Fern
Autumn Brown
Silver
Seminole Green
Bright Red
Warm Brown Antiquing Gel
Clear Satin Varnish

FACE, NECK, AND HANDS: Fleshtone, with a small amount of Sweetheart Blush blended into the cheeks, tip of nose, and mouth area.

EYES: White base. Then paint a dot of Blue Heaven in the center, corner or top of eye. Next, paint a smaller dot of black in the blue dot. Finally, use a toothpick and put a white highlight on the edge of the black dot. In the section where I paint the carving project, I'll go into more detail on placing the highlight, depending on where the eye is looking.

HAIR, GOATEE AND EYEBROWS: White

COAT AND BRIM OF HAT: Navy Blue

VEST: Antique Gold

BUTTONS ON VEST: Black

ICE SKATES: Silver or Pewter Grey

SHOES: Black

STRIPES ON HAT AND ON PANTS LEGS: Alternating Napthol Red and White

STARS ON HAT: White

BOWTIE: Napthol Red

Some patterns in the book may have specific colors in some areas. Where these colors are required, I have included them on the pattern.

Some patterns also have specific requirements, such as a base to support the weathervane, or the rocket rider. I have included the required information or directions on the pattern.

Patterns

Ready for the 4th

Carve the right hand as part of the main body. Use the hand template as an aid in drawing and carving the left hand.(Similar to Hand #7 on the template). You may have to adjust the size of the hand to fit your carving.

The fireworks box is fashioned from a wood scrap which measures 1 3/8" x 5/8" x 3/8", as shown on the pattern. It may be carved and adjusted, if needed, to fit your carving. Paint it a wood color, and use a fine-tip permanent pen for the lettering.

The supporting base is also made from a piece of scrap wood. Paint or stain it as you desire, or similar to some of the bases in the book. I normally put most of my Uncle Sams on bases so they will be more stable.

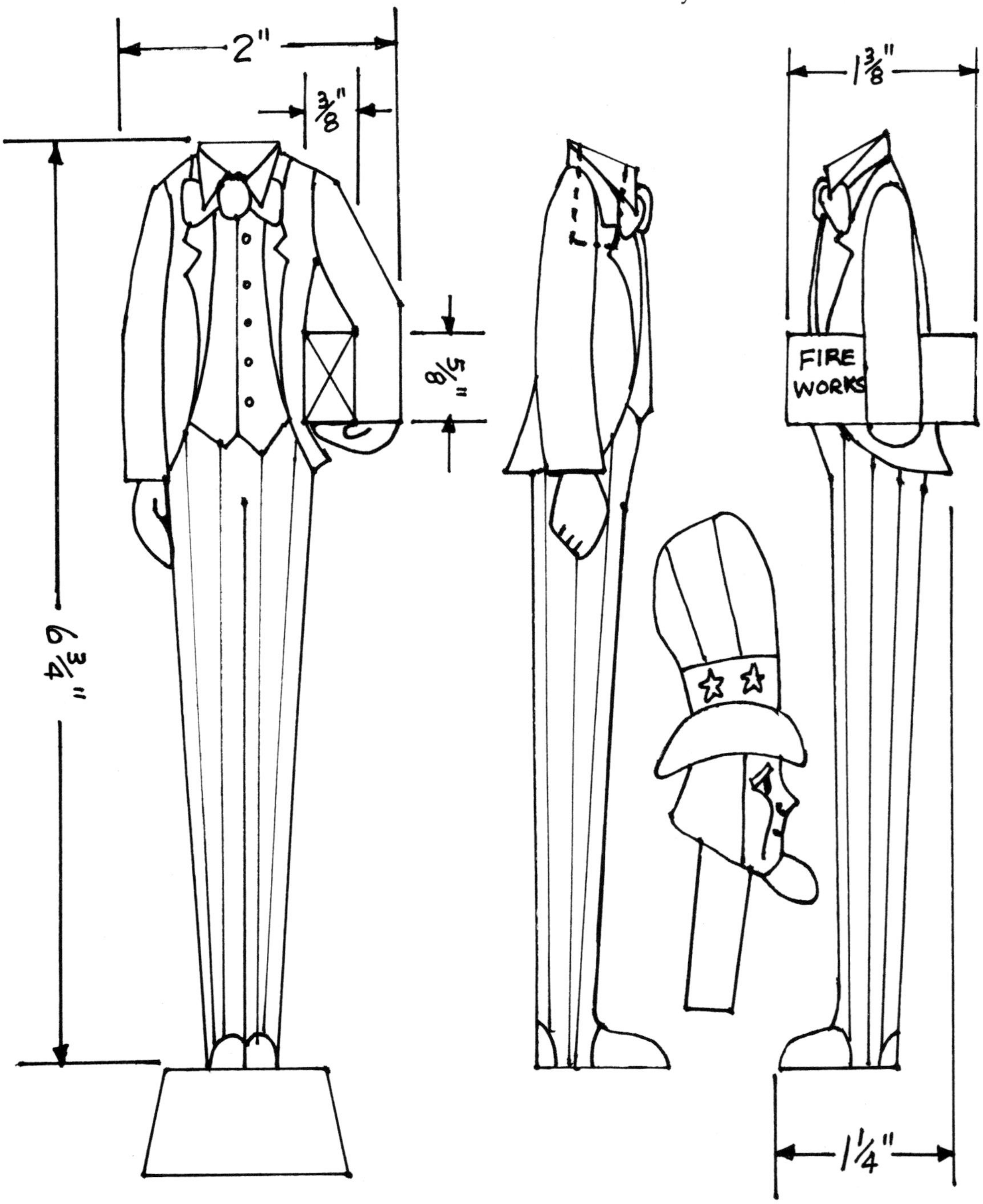

Enlarge 120% for original size.

Rocket's Away

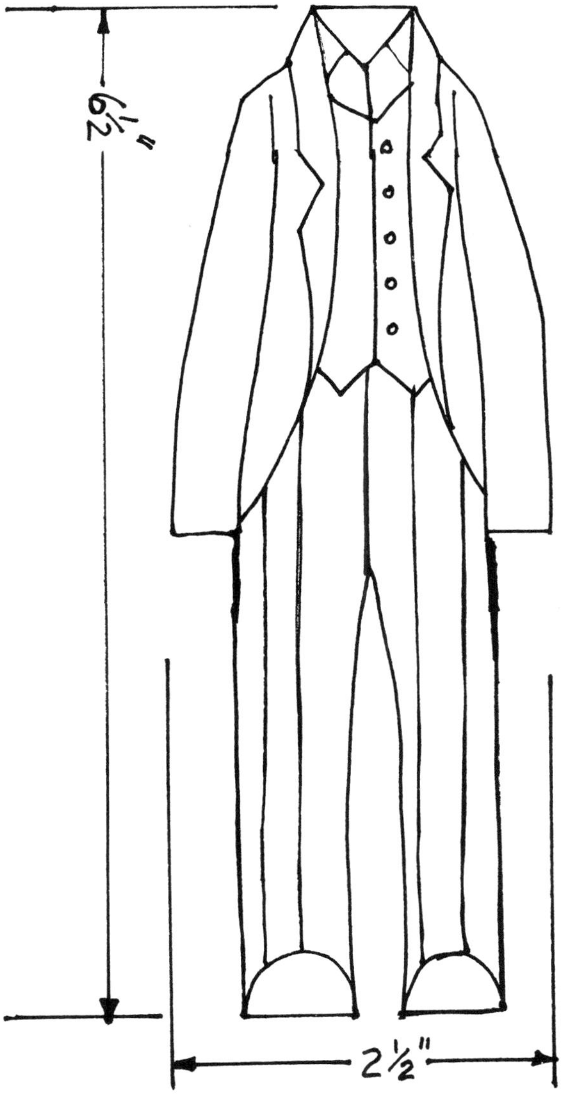

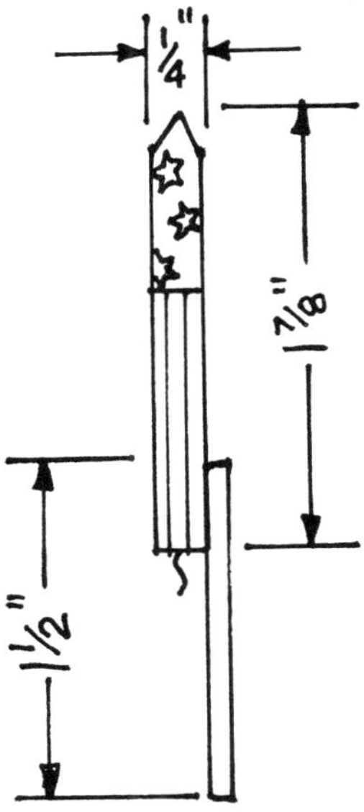

Use the hand template for both hands on this carving. Make sure the opening in the hand is 1/4" so the rockets will fit. (You will need to make two of these). These hands are similar to Hand #11 on the template. You may have to adjust the size of the hand to fit your carving. It is easiest if you saw out the top and side hand profiles, drill the necessary hole through the hand for a flag pole or rocket, etc., then finish carving and shaping the hand.

The main part of the rocket is fashioned from a 1/4" wood dowel. The small stick on the back is fashioned from a square toothpick with the sharp ends cut off.

Drill a small hole in the end of the rocket. Insert a short piece of heavy black thread, or a small piece of thin wire painted black.

Paint the rocket(s) as shown in the book, or a color of your choice.

Make a base of your choice to support the carving. Stain or paint it as desired.

Enlarge 120% for original size.

Gone Fishin'

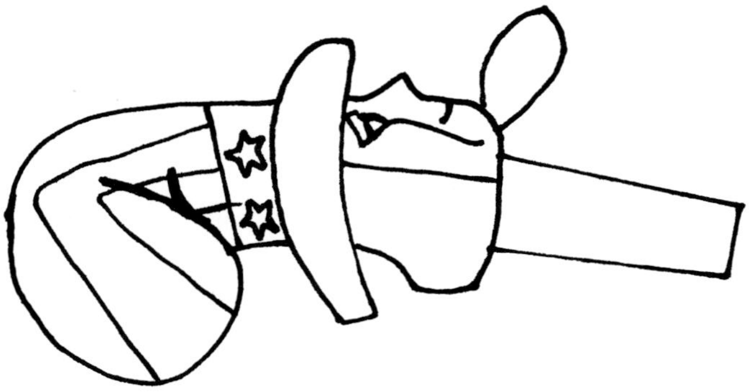

Use the hand template for both hands on this carving. The right hand will need a 1/8" opening in it to hold the fishing pole. These hands are similar to Hand #1 on the template. You may have to adjust the size of the hands to fit your carving. It is easiest if you saw out the top and side hand profiles, drill the necessary hole through the hand for a flag pole or rocket, etc., then finish carving and shaping the hand.

The fishing pole is made from a 1/8" wood dowel, cut to a length of your choice.

The fish line is a piece of heavy black thread.

Paint colors for the fish are:

BELLY: Pearl

SIDES: Boston Fern

TOP: Dark Forest Green

Glue the fish to one end of the thread, and glue the other end of the thread to the pole.

The pole is painted Autumn Brown.

Since this figure is seated, no base is really necessary. Make one if you desire.

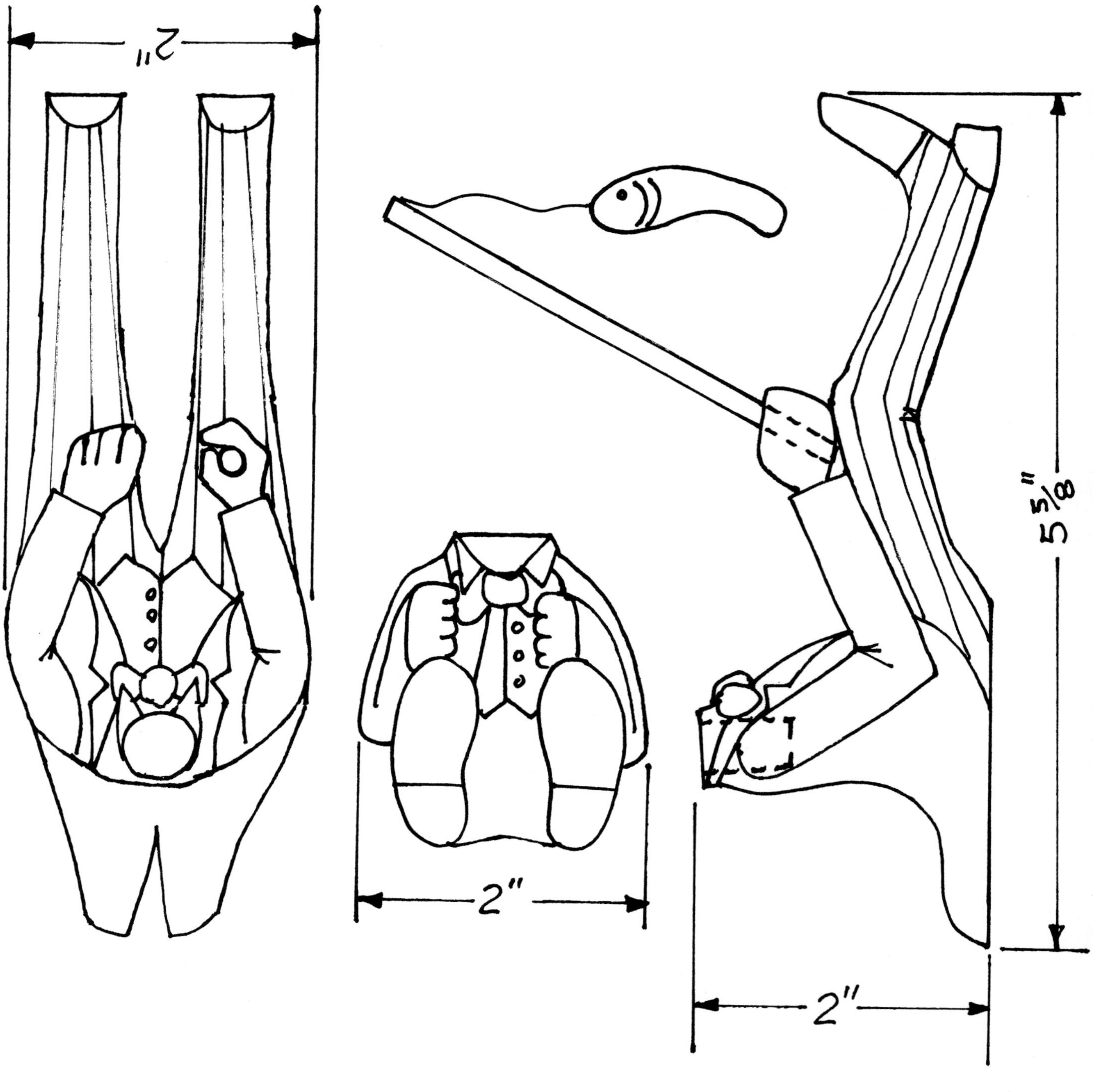

Ice Skating Sam

Carve the hands as part of the body.

The skates are painted Silver.

This figure will require a base. Cut a small slot in the base, big enough to fit the bottom of the skate. Glue the skate into the slot, and support the figure until the glue dries.

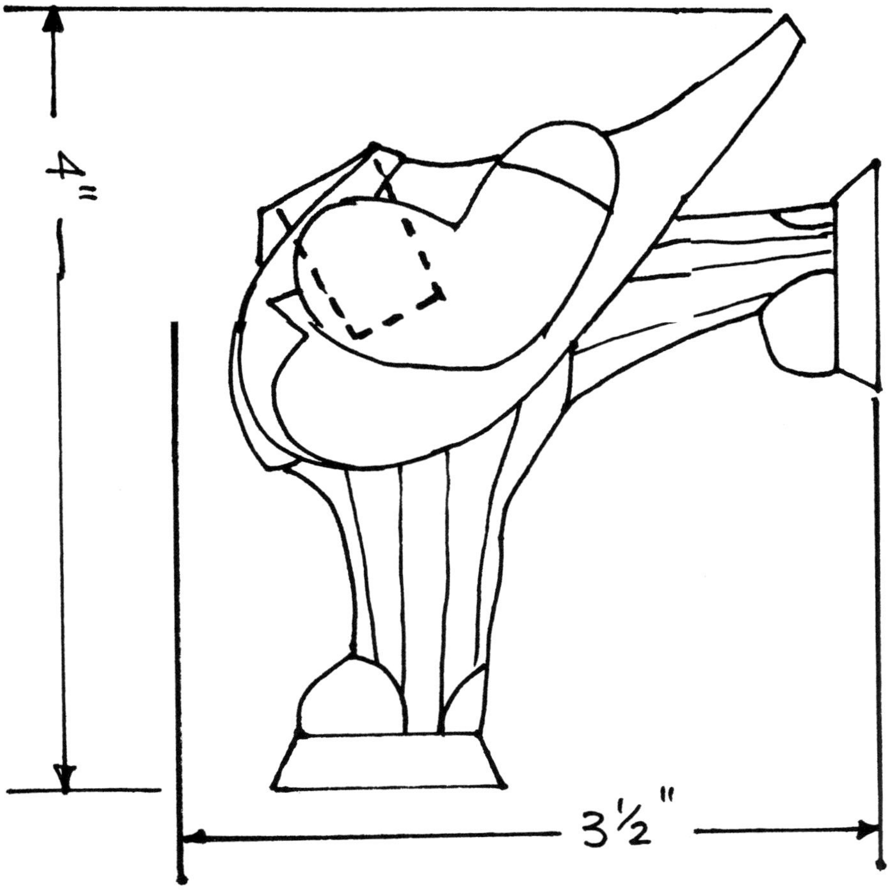

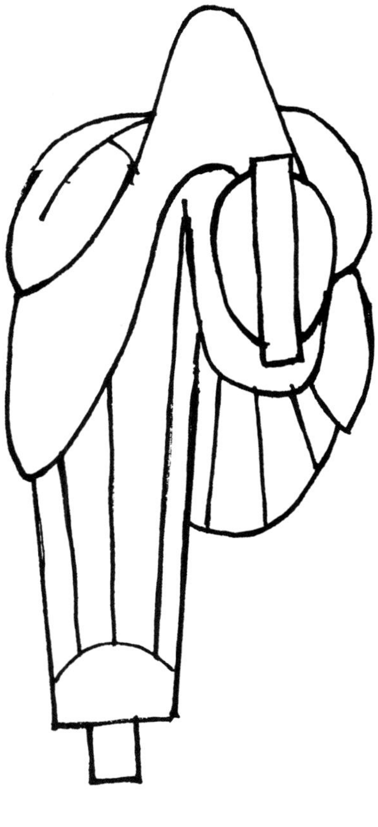

Flag Waver #1

Hands may be carved as part of the body, or you may use the hand template. The hands will need 1/8" holes through them to hold the flag poles. These hands are similar to Hand #2 on the template. You may have to adjust the size of the hand to fit your carving. It is easiest if you saw out the top and side hand profiles, drill the necessary hole through the hand for a flag pole or rocket, etc., then finish carving and shaping the hand.

Two flags and flag poles are needed for this carving. The poles are made from 1/8" wood dowels, and the flag portion is made from a 1/8" Basswood sheet (you can find these sheets at hobby and craft stores). Glue the flag to the dowel, and cut the dowel to a length you desire (or use the length on the pattern as a guide).

Paint the flag poles Antique Gold.

The main body consists of two parts: **Part "A"** is made from a 1/8" Basswood sheet. **Part "B"** is made from Basswood or similar. Leave a small, flat section in the center of the coat when carving. When the body is carved, glue Part "A" to the back of the coat as shown.

Make a base of your choice, if desired.

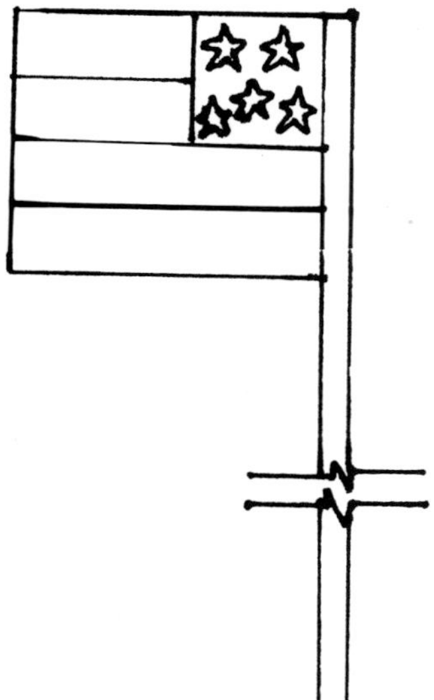

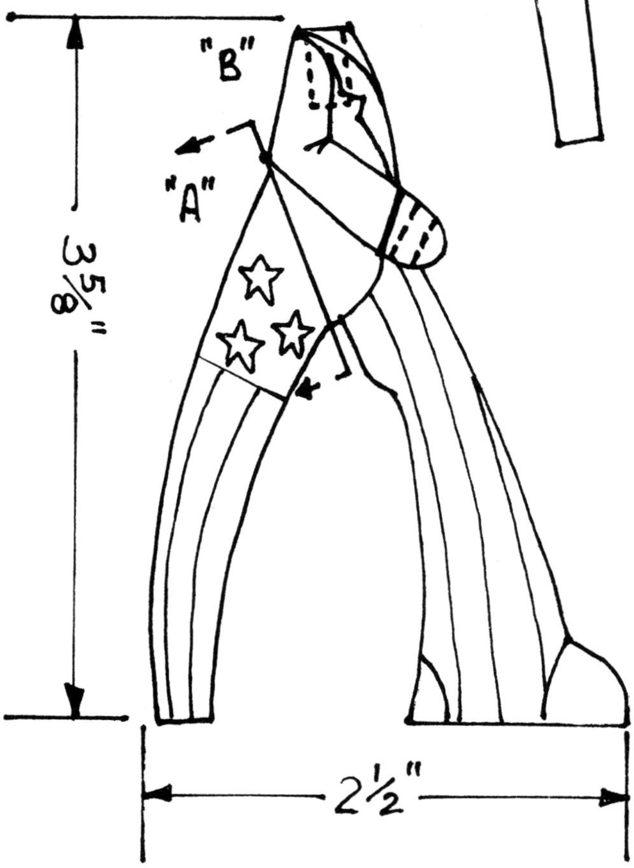

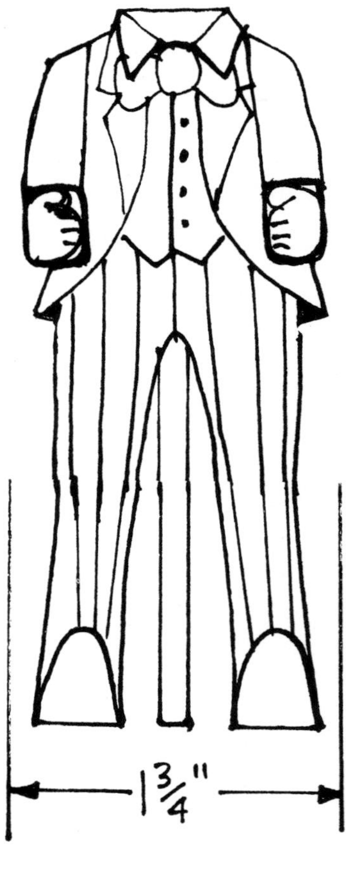

Roly-Poly Sam

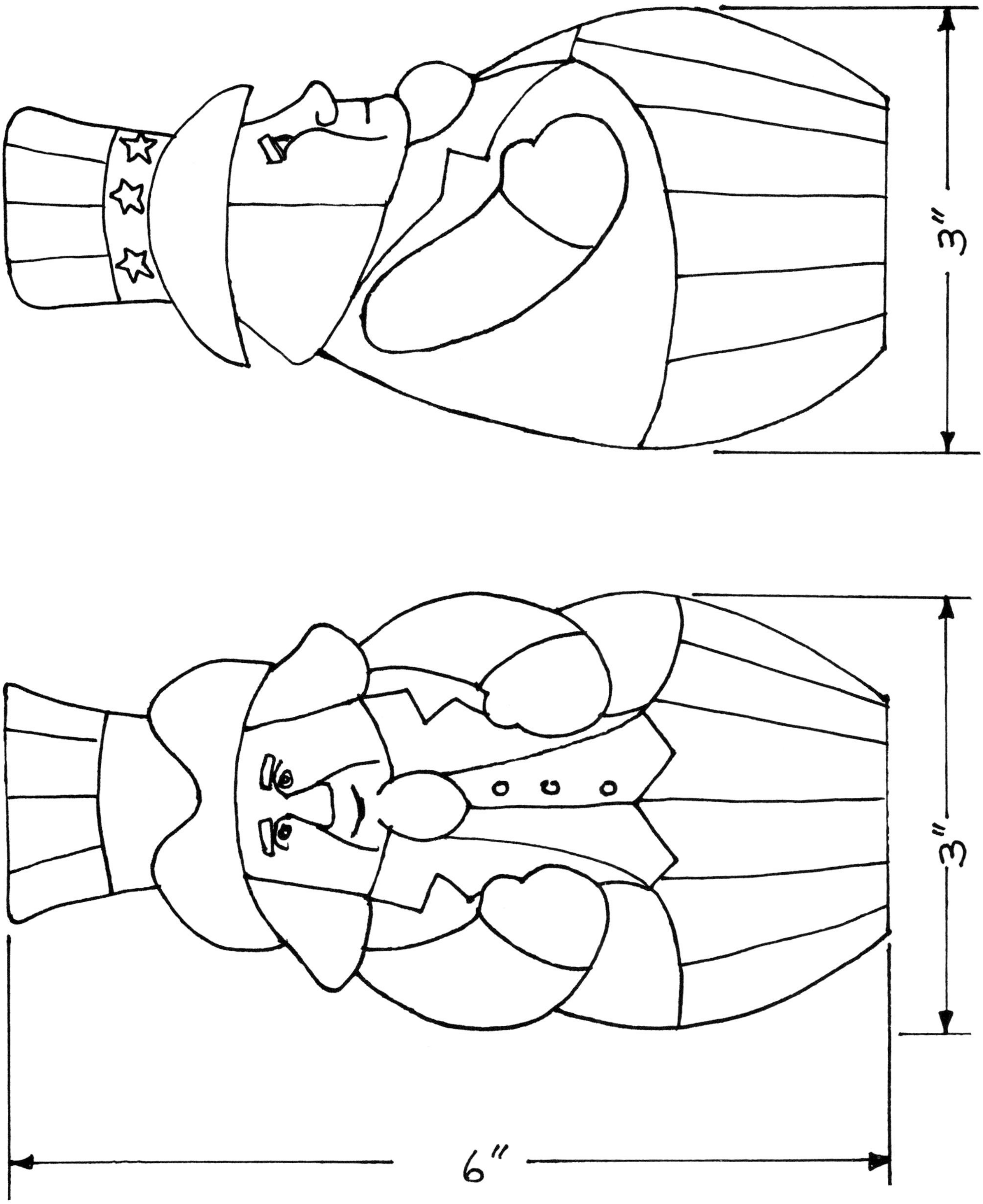

Bungee Jumper/Fan Pull

Carve the hands as part of the body.

When the project is carved, painted and assembled, put a small screw eye hook in the top of the hat. Attach a small piece of elastic string to the screw eye, and attach the other end of the elastic to a doorway or fireplace mantle. A slight pull on Uncle Sam's feet will start him "jumping".

To use him as a fan or light pull, use a piece of heavy string instead of elastic string.

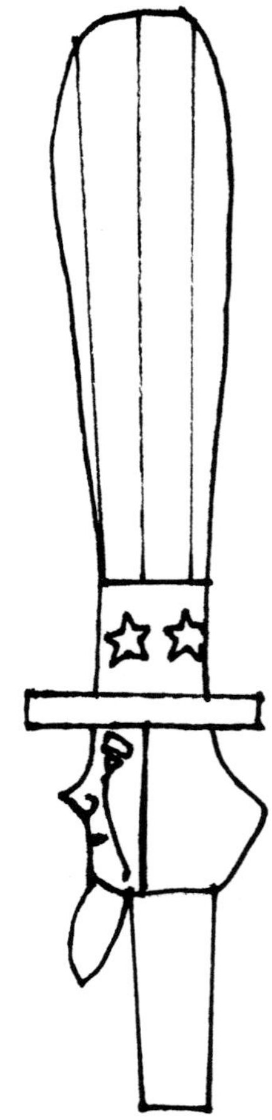

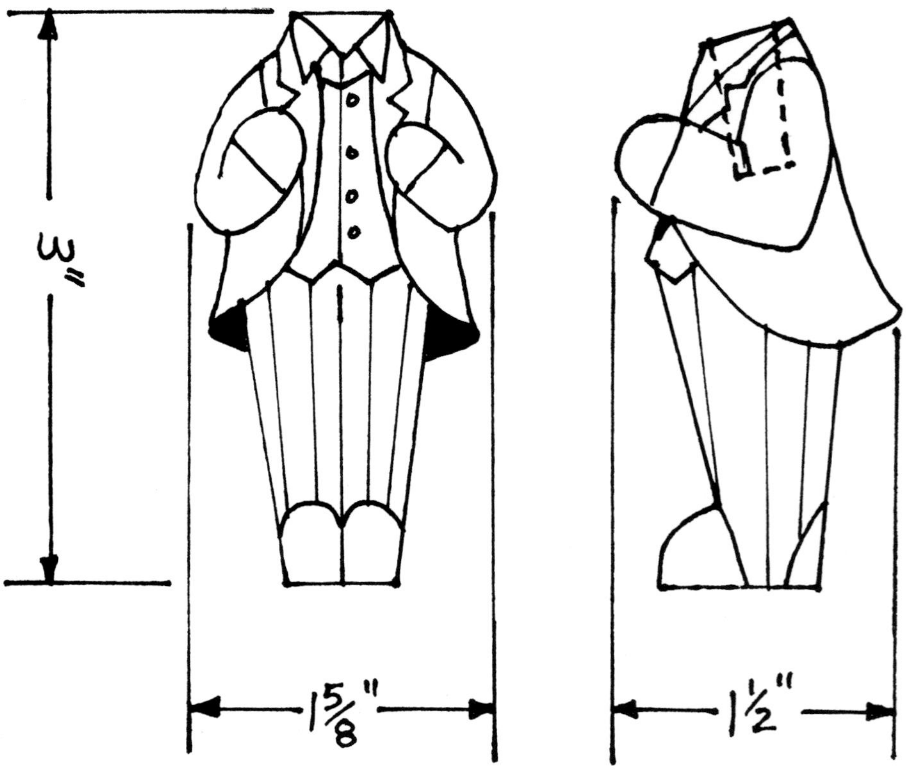

Sams-in-the-Moon

Use 3/4" wood for these patterns.

Carve one side of the wood only.

Attach a screw eye hook in the top of the hat. Put a piece of string through the eye hook so the Sams-In-The-Moon can be used as ornaments.

Paint the moon part of the carving Antique Gold.

Paint the other part of the carving as suggested in the general painting section.

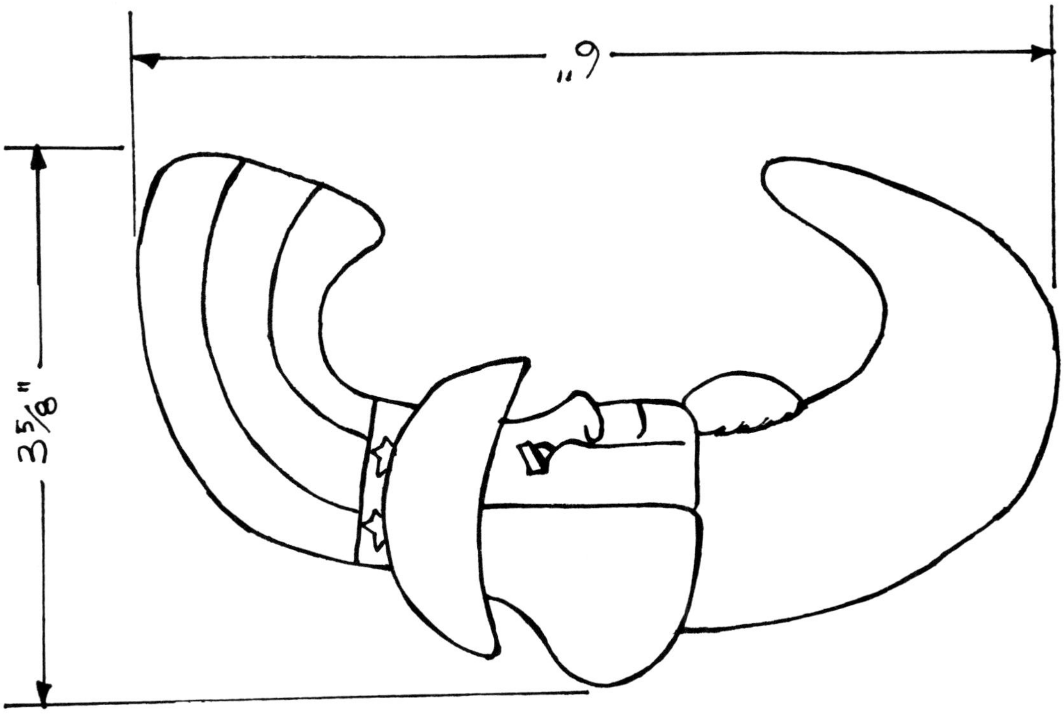

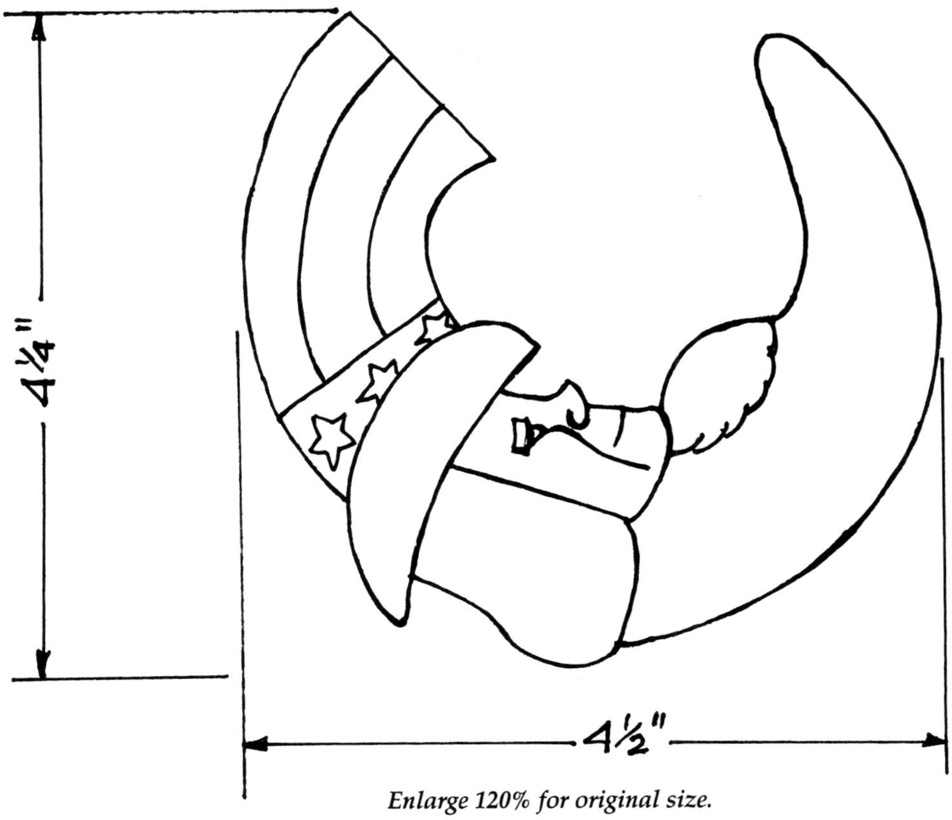

Enlarge 120% for original size.

Weathervane

Use 3/4" wood for this pattern.

Carve both sides the same; then drill a 1/4" hole through the hands as shown.

Make the firecracker from a piece of 1/4" wood dowel. Put a small hole in one end of it, and insert a short piece of heavy black thread. A small piece of wire, painted Black, may be used instead of thread.

Firecracker colors:

Upper part: NAVY Blue, with White stars.

Lower part: Alternating stripes of Napthol Red and White.

Drill a 5/16" hole in Uncle Sam's belly. Make a supporting base of your choice, with a 5/16" hole drilled in it. Use a short piece of 5/16" wood dowel to connect Uncle Sam to the base.

Stain or paint the base and dowel a color of your choice.

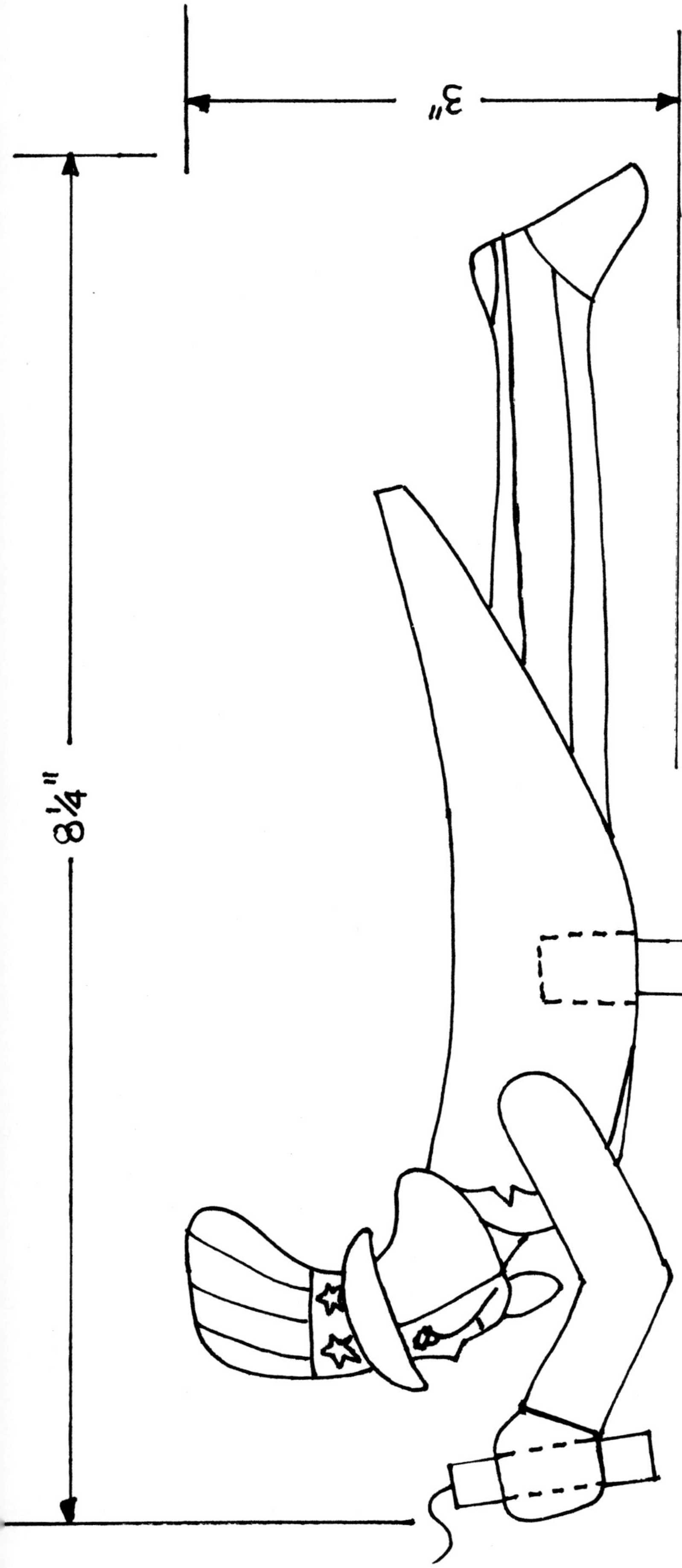

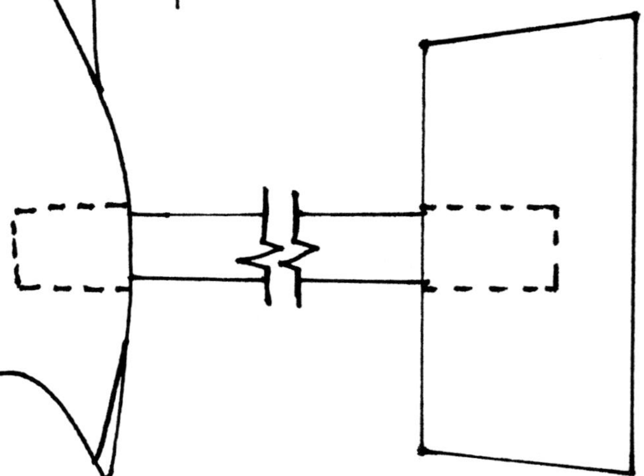

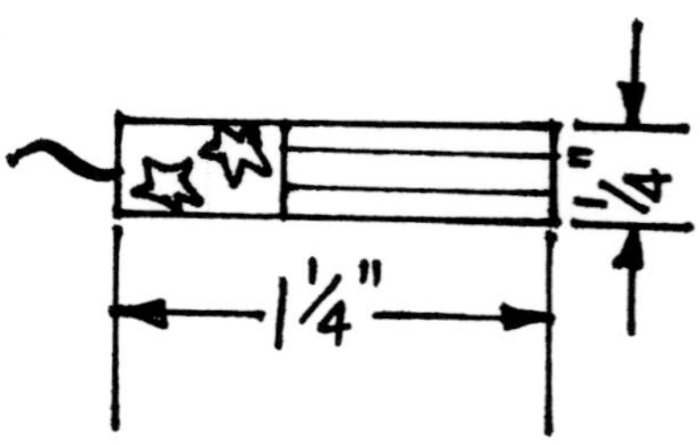

Shelf Sitter

Whirligig

Drill a 1/4" hole through the body where you see the "+" on the body pattern.

Make two arms, and drill 1/4" holes through them as shown by the "+" on the arm pattern.

Carve and paint the body, arms and head.

Glue the head in place first, positioned as you want it. Next, use your drill and re-bore the 1/4" hole through the body, so the neck inside the body will also have the hole through it. Insert a 1/4" wood dowel through the body, and cut it so that approximately 1/2" is exposed on each side of the body. Put a small drop of glue on one dowel end, and place the arm over it. Slide the arm close to the body, but not quite touching. Do the same thing for the other arm, but make sure the other arm is pointing in a direction opposite of the first arm you installed. When the glue is dry, trim away any excess dowel protruding from the outside edge of the arms, and paint the area the same color as the coat. The arms should rotate freely when you give them a spin.

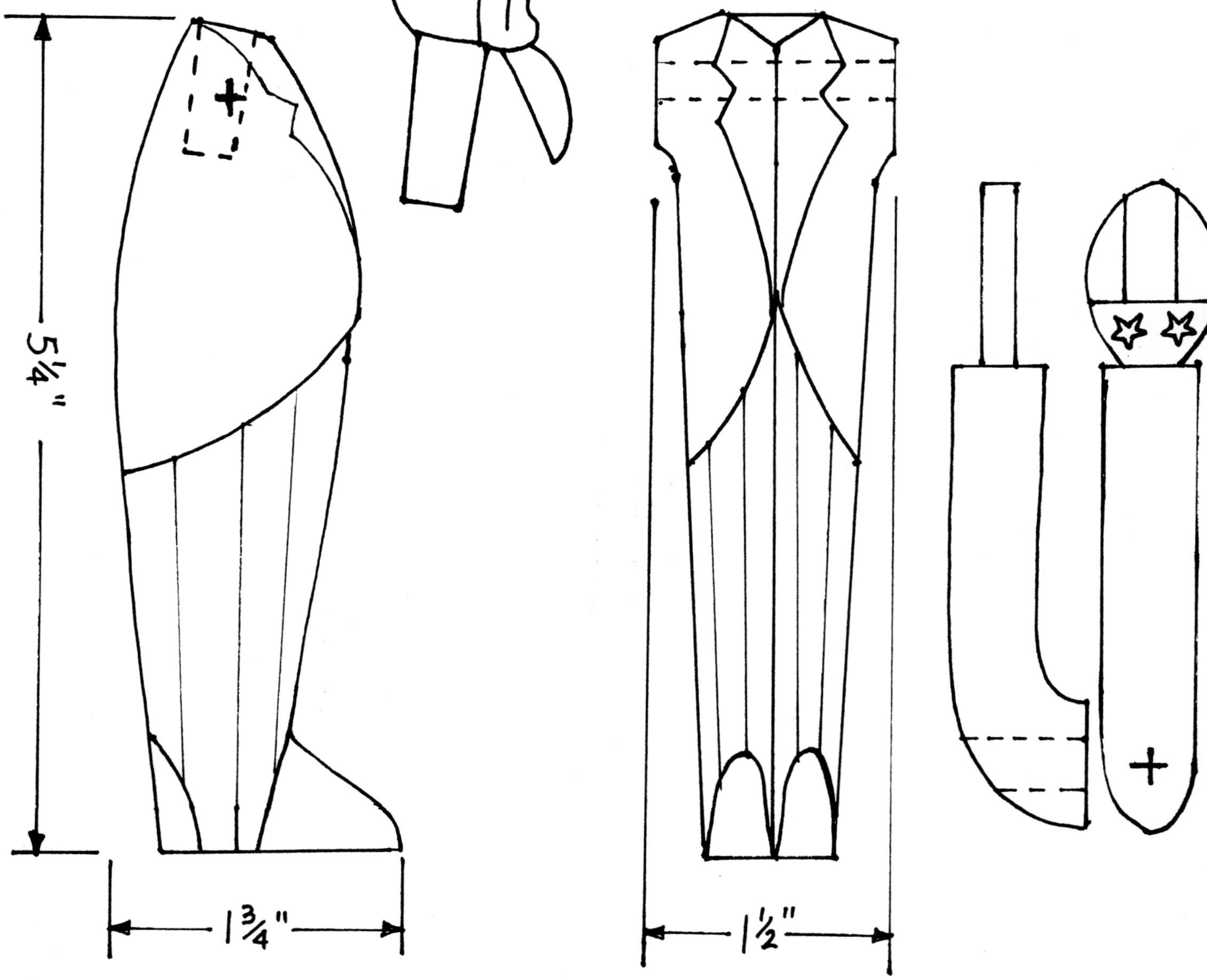

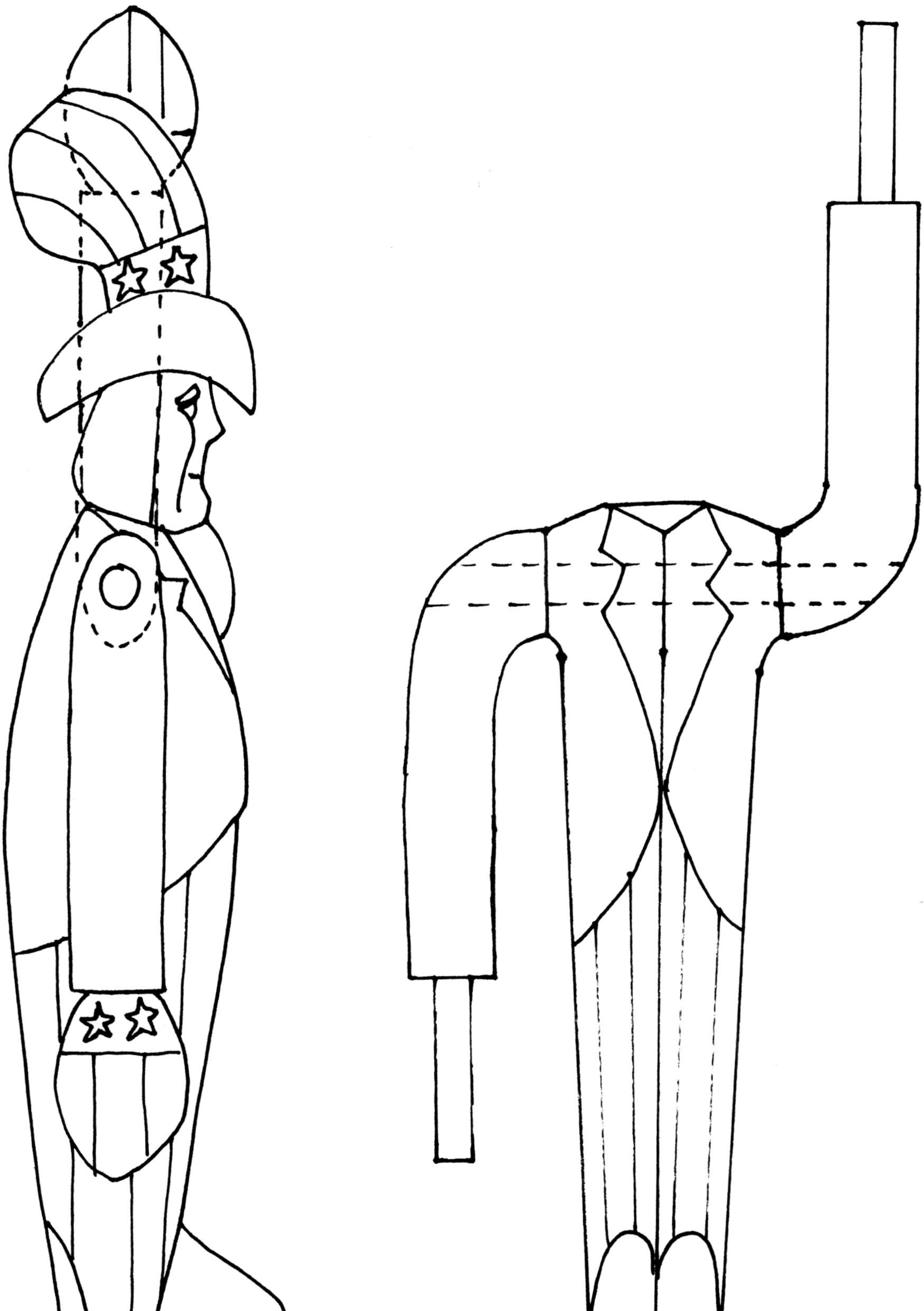

Rocket Ridin' Sam

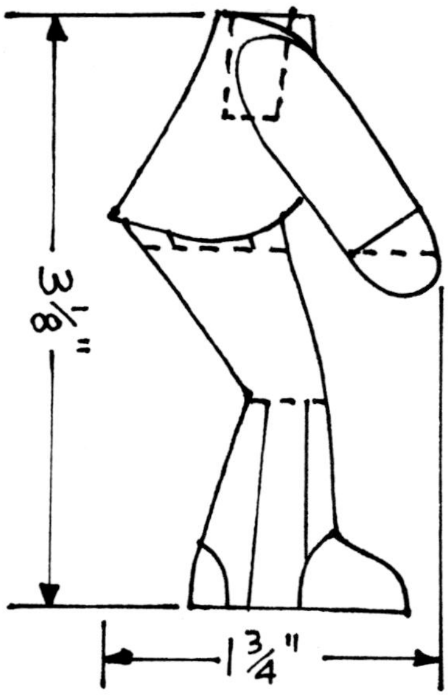

The hands are carved as part of the body.

After sawing out the pattern, drill a 3/4" hole through the arms and legs as shown on the pattern.

Make the rocket from a piece of 3/4" wood dowel. The stick at the back of the rocket is made from a scrap piece of wood, 1/4" square by three inches long. Also drill a 1/4" hole into the rocket at approximately the angle shown on the pattern.

Once you have carved and painted the project, slide the rocket through Uncle Sam's legs from the back side, and glue it in place.

Make a base of your choice, with a 1/4" hole drilled in it. Use a piece of 1/4" wood dowel to connect Uncle Sam to the base.

The rocket is painted similar to the firecrackers in the other patterns. The fuse is made from a piece of heavy Black thread, or small piece of wire painted Black, and inserted into a hole drilled into the back of the rocket.

Stain or paint the dowel and base a color of your choice.

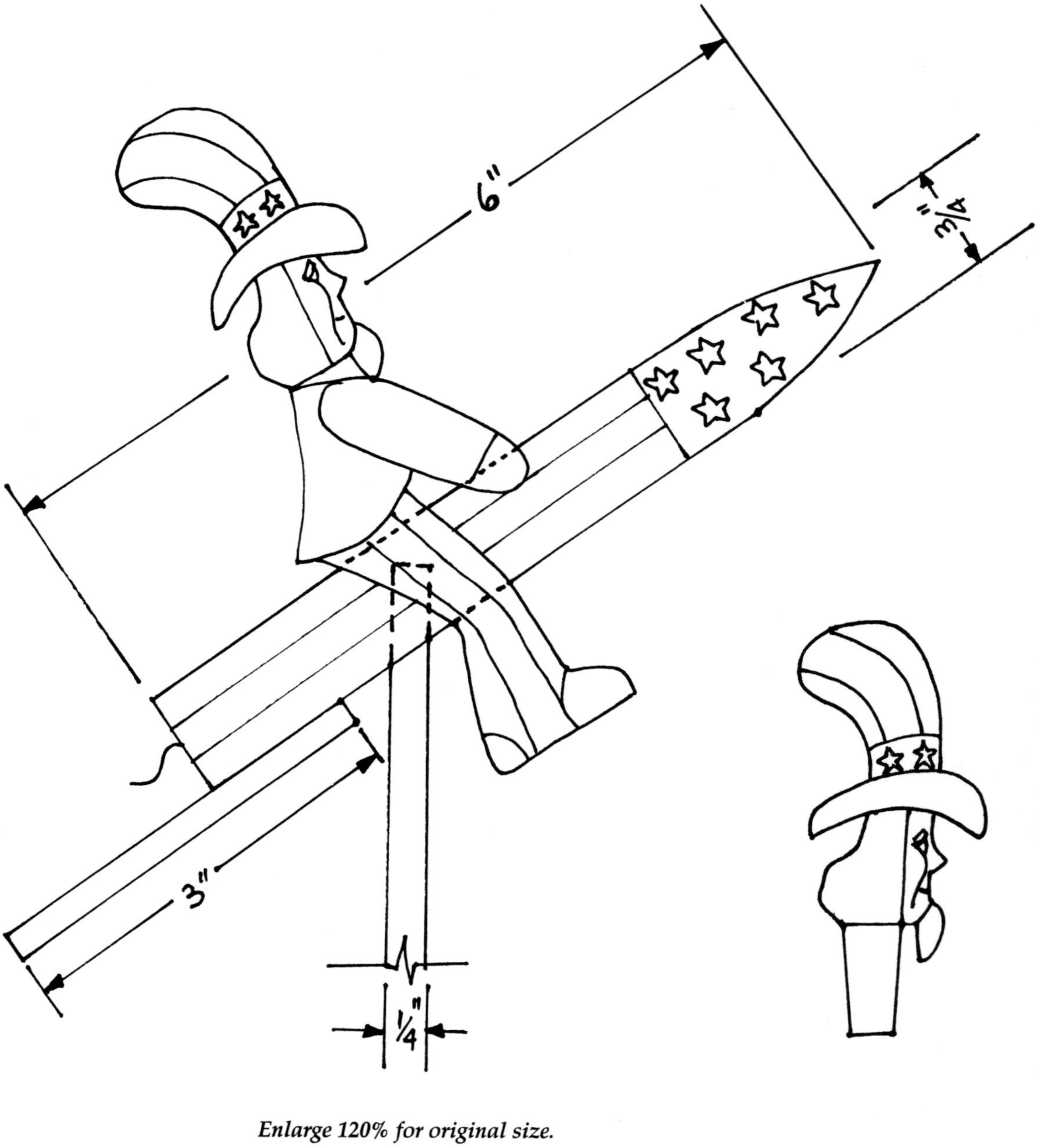

Enlarge 120% for original size.

I Want You

Carve the left hand as part of the body. The hand is similar to Hand #6 on the template. You may have to adjust the size of the hand to fit your carving.

You will probably need to make a base for this project, to give it stability.

Tripod Sam #1

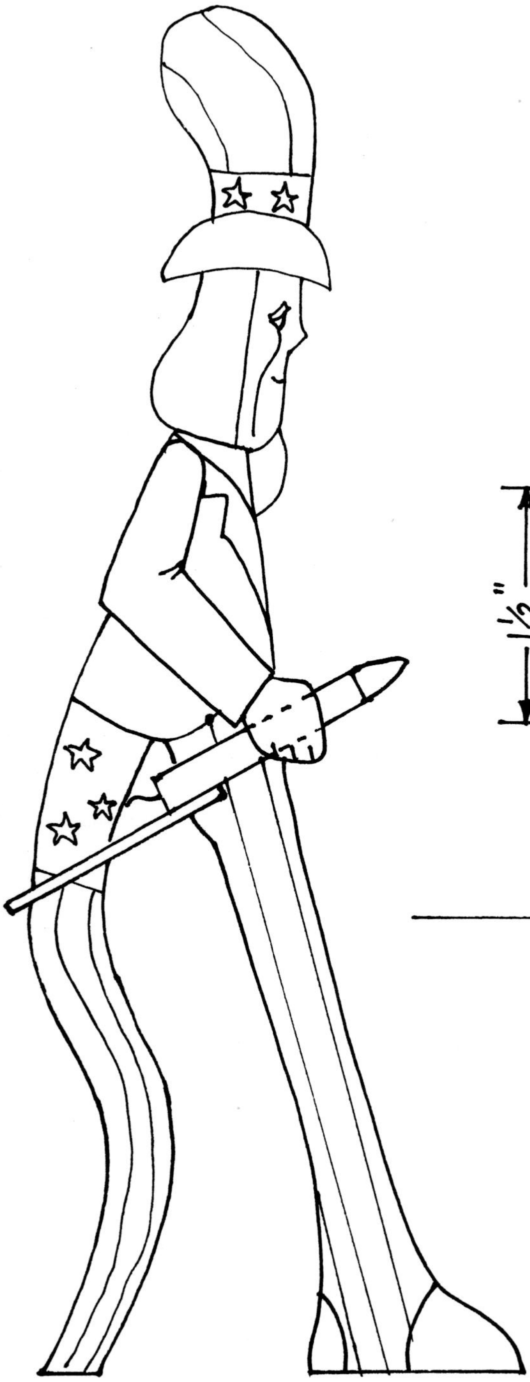

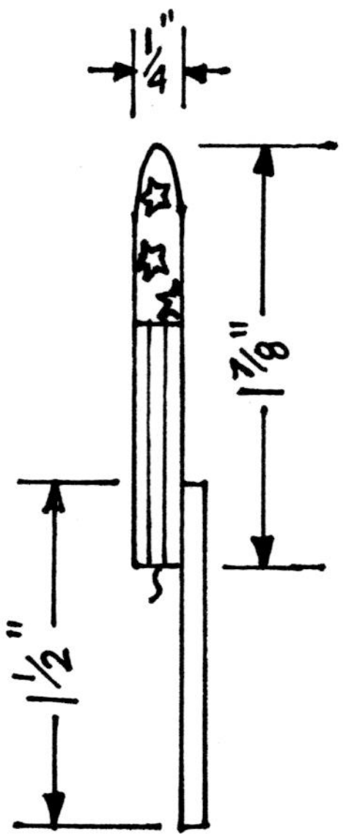

Hands may be carved as part of the body, or you may use the hand template. The hands will need 1/4" holes through them to hold the skyrockets. These hands are similar to Hand #2 on the template. You may have to adjust the size of the hand to fit your carving. It is easiest if you saw out the top and side hand profiles, drill the necessary hole through the hand for a flag pole or rocket, etc., then finish carving and shaping the hand.

Two skyrockets are needed for this carving. They are made from 1/4" wood dowels, and the stick portion at the back is made from a square toothpick with the sharp ends cut off. The fuse is made from a piece of heavy Black thread, or small piece of wire painted Black, and inserted into a hole drilled into the back of the rocket.

The main body consists of two parts: **Part "A"** is made from a 1/8" Basswood sheet. **Part "B"** is made from Basswood or similar. Leave a small, flat section in the center of the coat when carving. When the body is carved, glue Part "A" to the back of the coat as shown.

Make a base of your choice, if desired.

Paint the skyrockets similar to the firecrackers in other patterns.

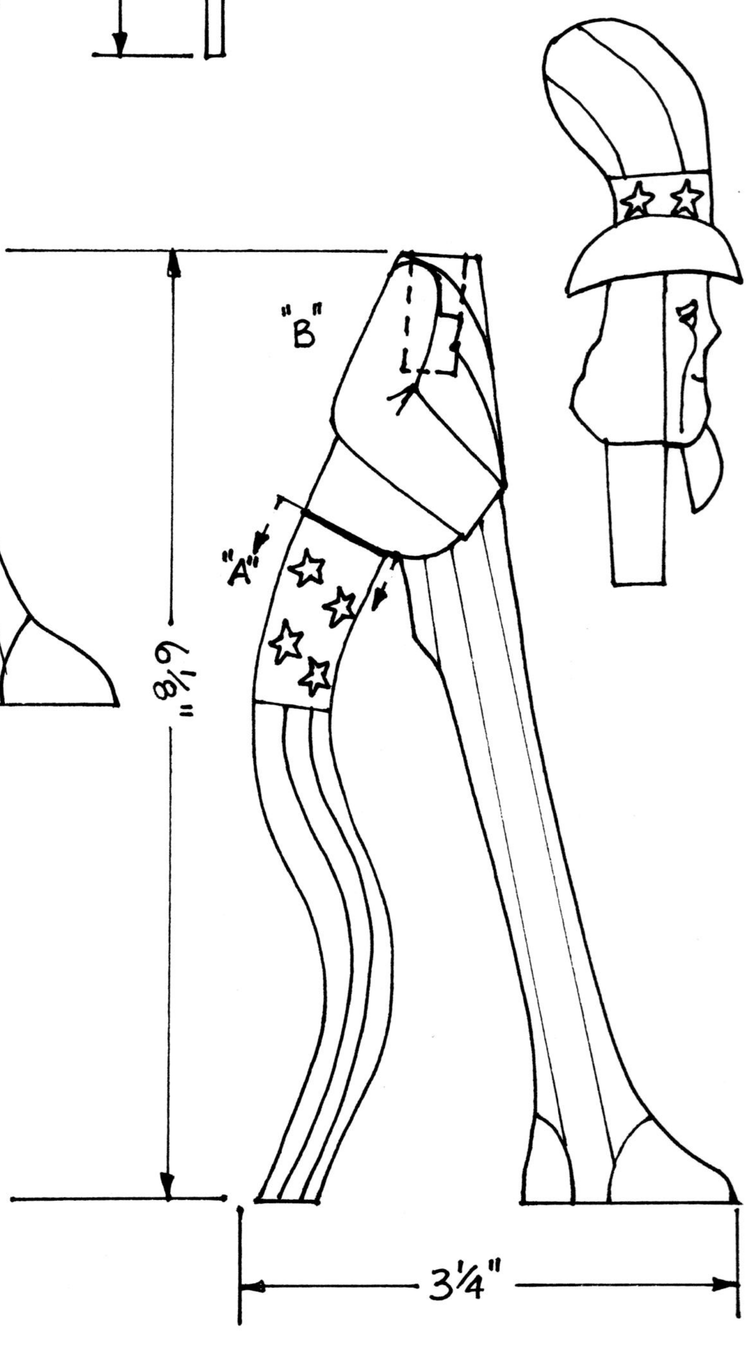

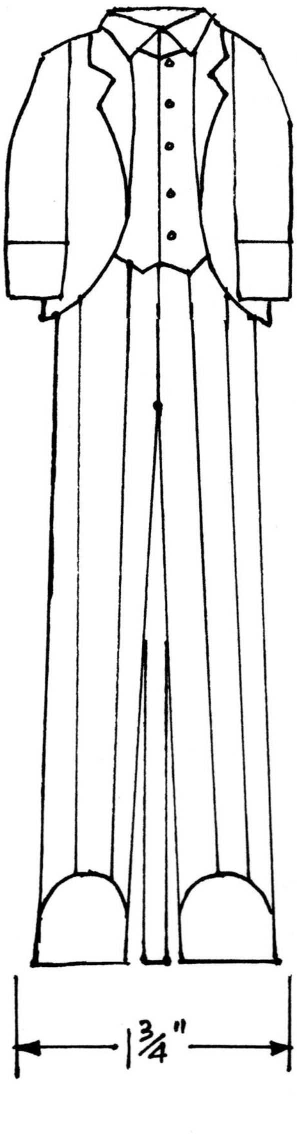

Enlarge 120% for original size.

Eatin' Watermelon

Use the hand template for the hands.These hands are similar to Hand #8 on the template. You may have to adjust the size of the hands to fit your carving.

The watermelon is made from a scrap piece of wood 1/4" x 2".

Paint the watermelon as follows:

Rind: Seminole Green
"Meat": Bright Red
Seeds: Black

After carving and painting all pieces, glue the melon slice in Uncle Sam's hands.

Make a base if desired, but this project doesn't really need one for support.

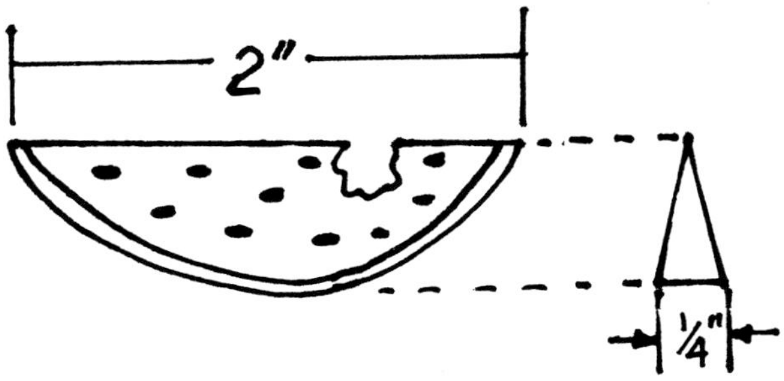

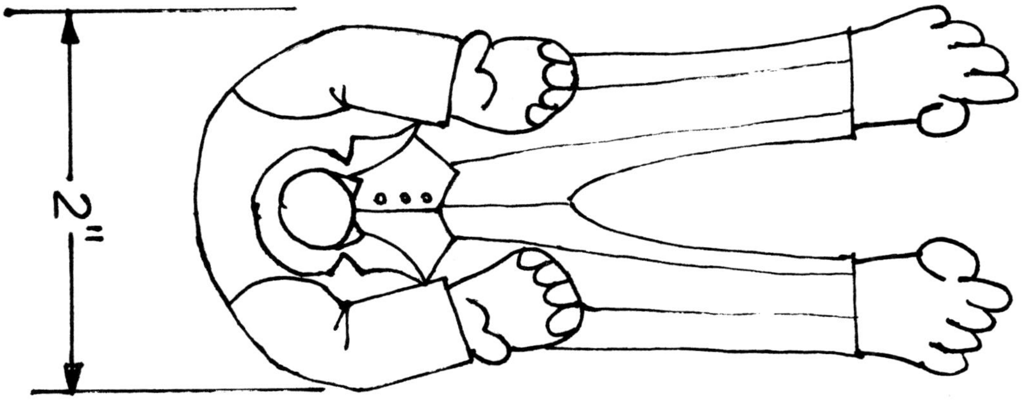

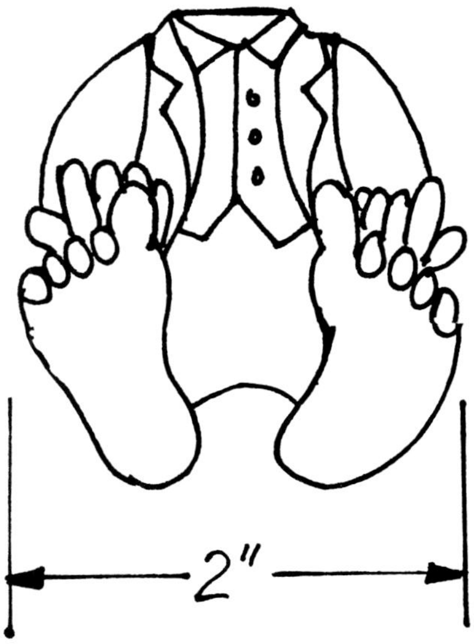

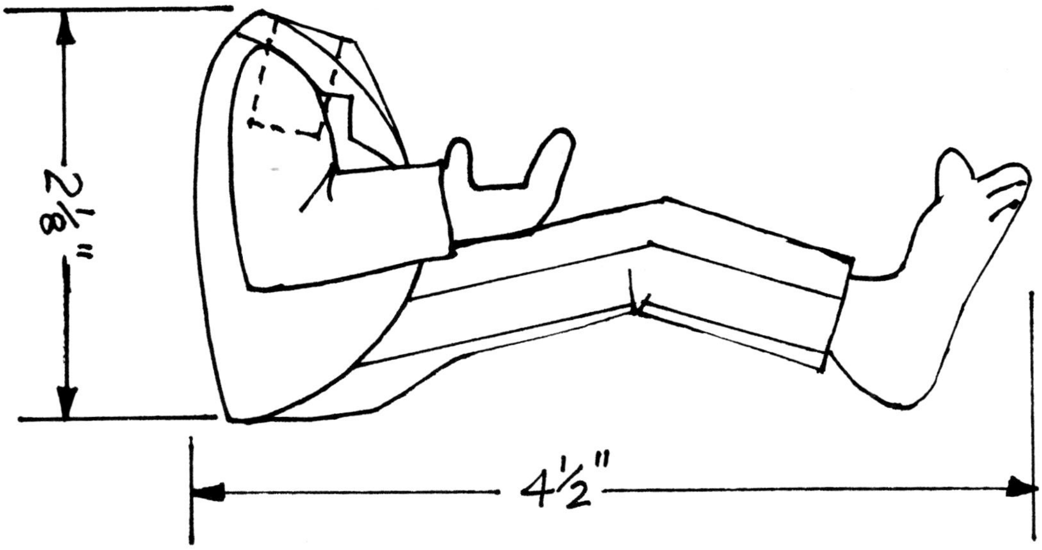

Star Sam

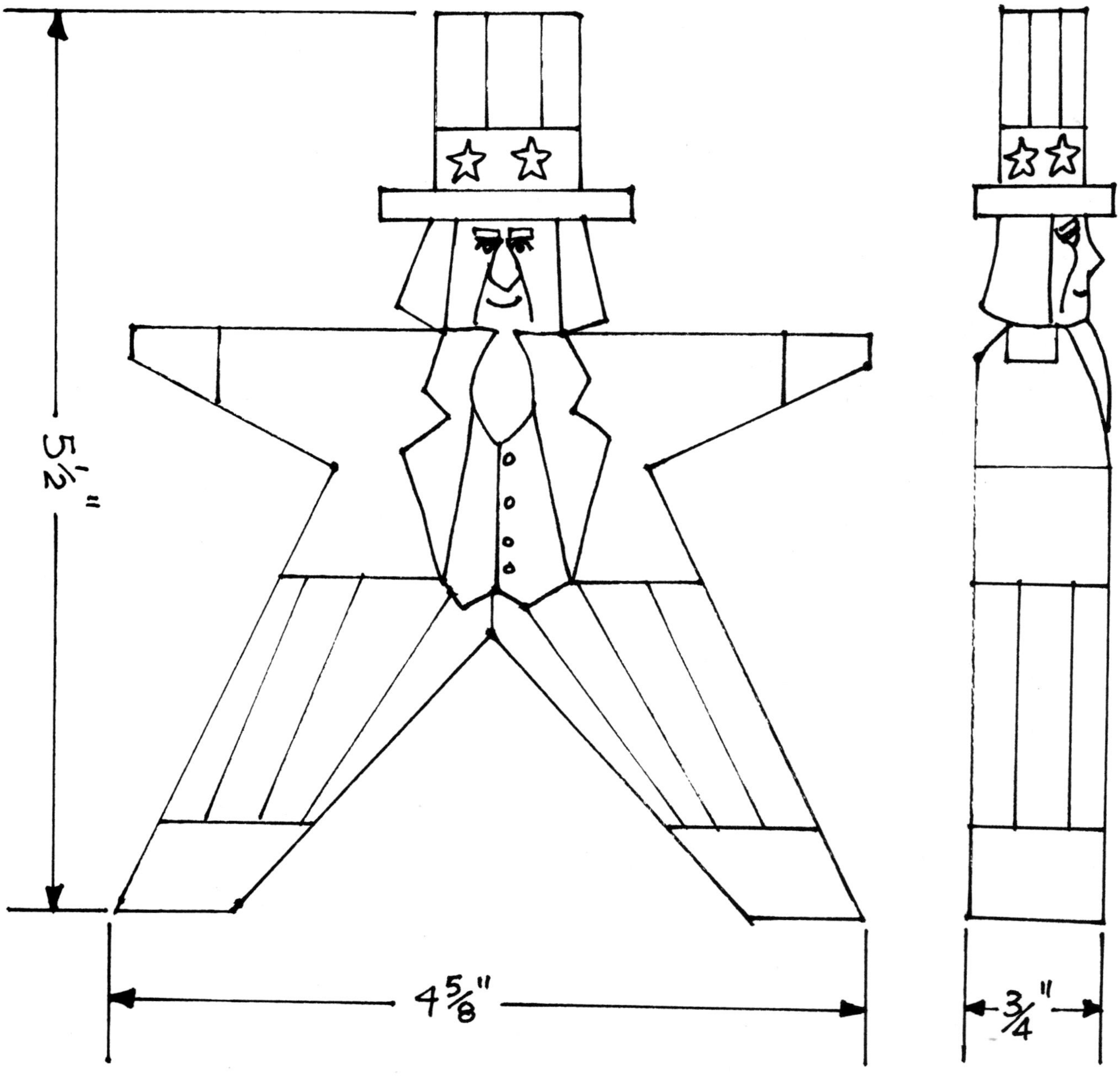

Flag Waver #2

Hands may be carved as part of the body, or you may use the hand template. The hands will need 1/8" holes through them to hold the flag poles. These hands are similar to Hand #1 on the template. You may have to adjust the size of the hand to fit your carving. It is easiest if you saw out the top and side hand profiles, drill the necessary hole through the hand for a flag pole or rocket, etc., then finish carving and shaping the hand.

Two flags and flag poles are needed for this carving. The poles are made from 1/8" wood dowels, and the flag portion is made from a 1/8" Basswood sheet (you can find these sheets at hobby and craft stores). Glue the flag to the dowel, and cut the dowel to a length you desire (or use the length on the pattern as a guide).

Paint the flag poles Antique Gold.

Drill a 5/16" hole in the bottom of the body. Make a base of your choice and drill a 5/16" hole in it. Use a piece of 5/16" dowel to connect the body to the base.

Stain or paint the dowel and base a color of your choice.

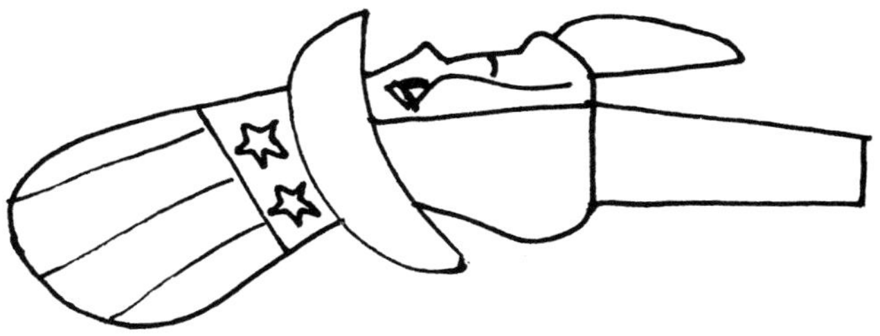

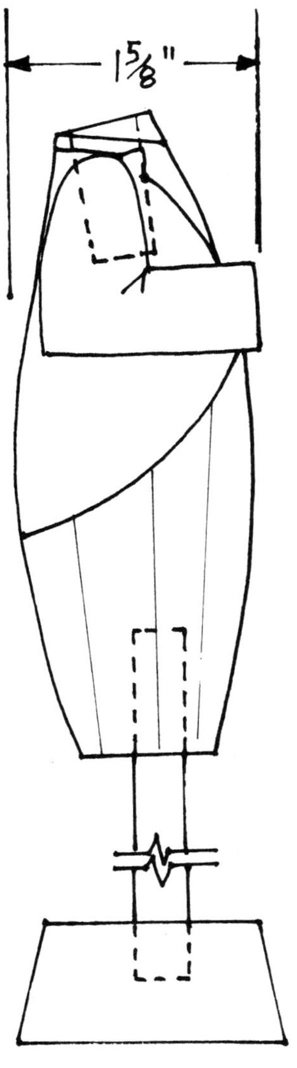

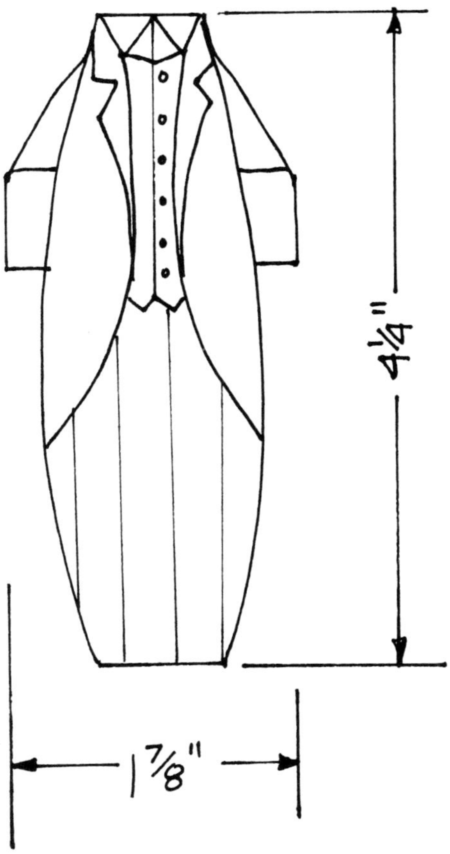

Enlarge 120% for original size.

Everything's Fine

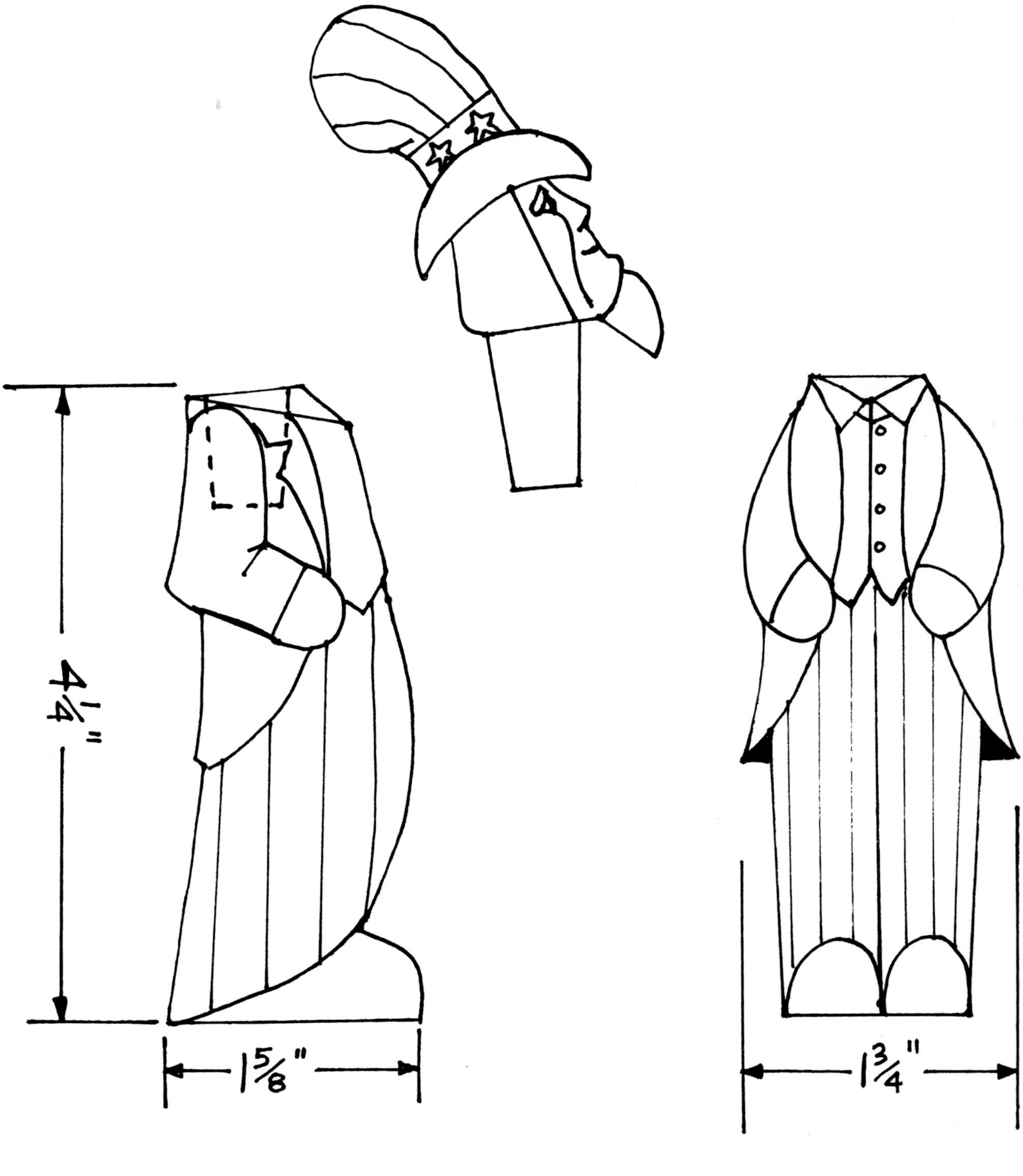

Ready for the 4th #2

Use the hand template for the hands. You will need 1/4" holes through the hands for the firecrackers. These hands are similar to Hand #12 on the template. You may have to adjust the size of the hand to fit your carving. It is easiest if you saw out the top and side hand profiles, drill the necessary hole through the hand for a flag pole or rocket, etc., then finish carving and shaping the hand.

Make two firecrackers from pieces of 1/4" wood dowels. The fuse is made from a piece of heavy Black thread, or small piece of wire painted Black, and inserted into a hole drilled into the top of the firecrackers.

Make a base for this project if desired, and paint or stain it as you wish.

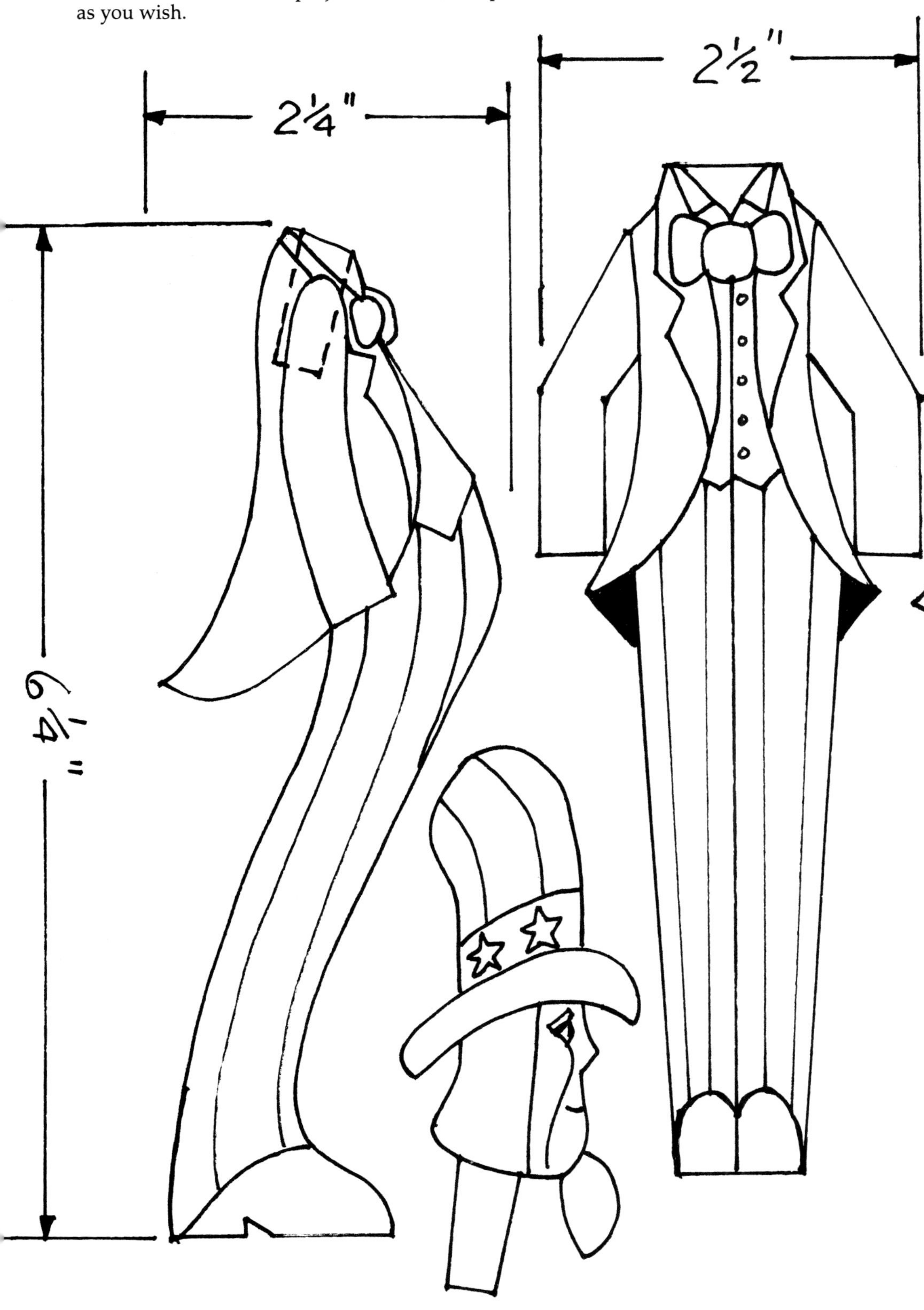

Tripod Sam #2

Hands may be carved as part of the body, or you may use the hand template. The hands will need 1/8" holes through them to hold the flag poles. These hands are similar to Hand #2 on the template. You may have to adjust the size of the hand to fit your carving. It is easiest if you saw out the top and side hand profiles, drill the necessary hole through the hand for a flag pole or rocket, etc., then finish carving and shaping the hand.

Two flags and flag poles are needed for this carving. The poles are made from 1/8" wood dowels, and the flag portion is made from a 1/8" Basswood sheet (you can find these sheets at hobby and craft stores). Glue the flag to the dowel, and cut the dowel to a length you desire (or use the length on the pattern as a guide).

Paint the flag poles Antique Gold.

The main body consists of two parts: **Part "A"** is made from a 1/8" Basswood sheet. **Part "B"** is made from Basswood or similar. Leave a small, flat section in the center of the coat when carving. When the body is carved, glue Part "A" to the back of the coat as shown.

Make a base of your choice, if desired.

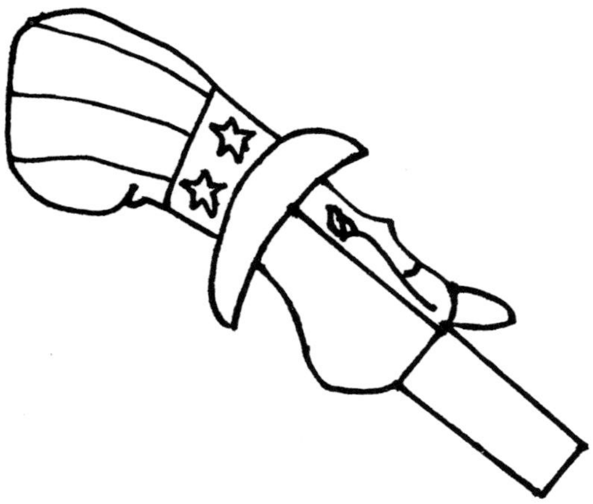

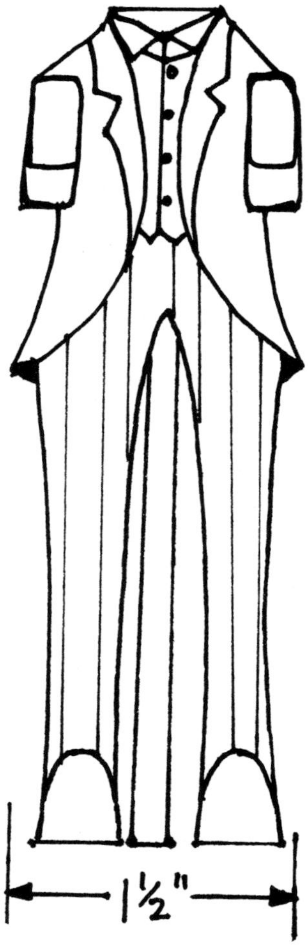

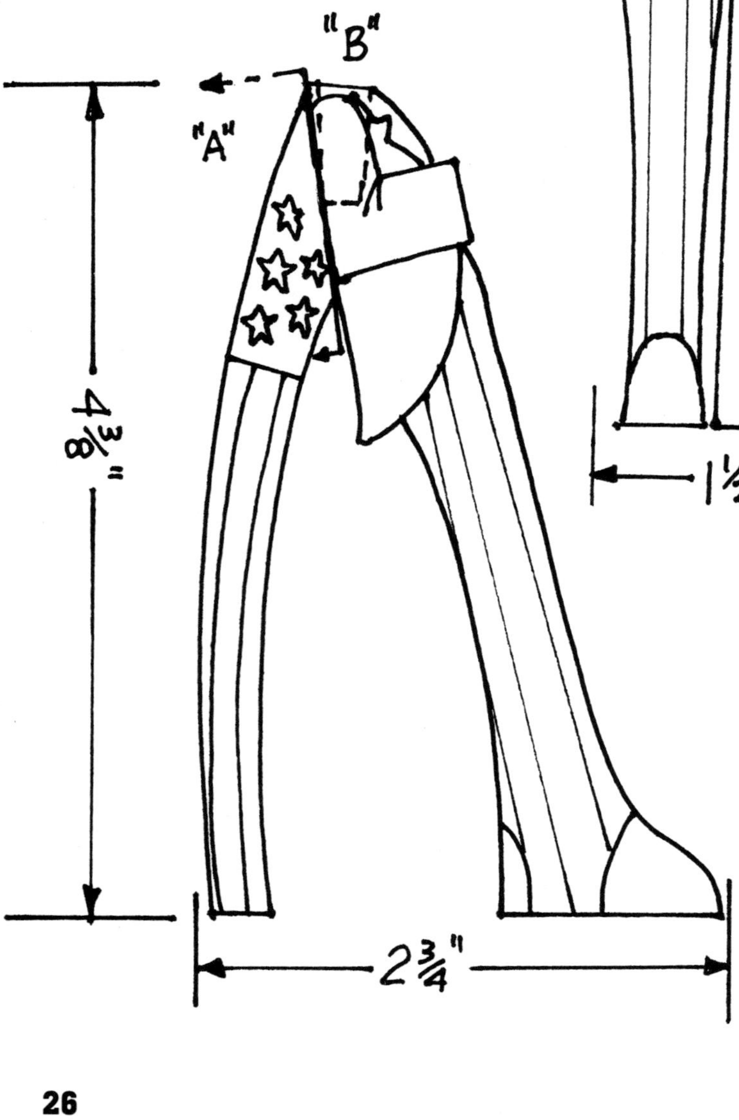

Laid Back Sam

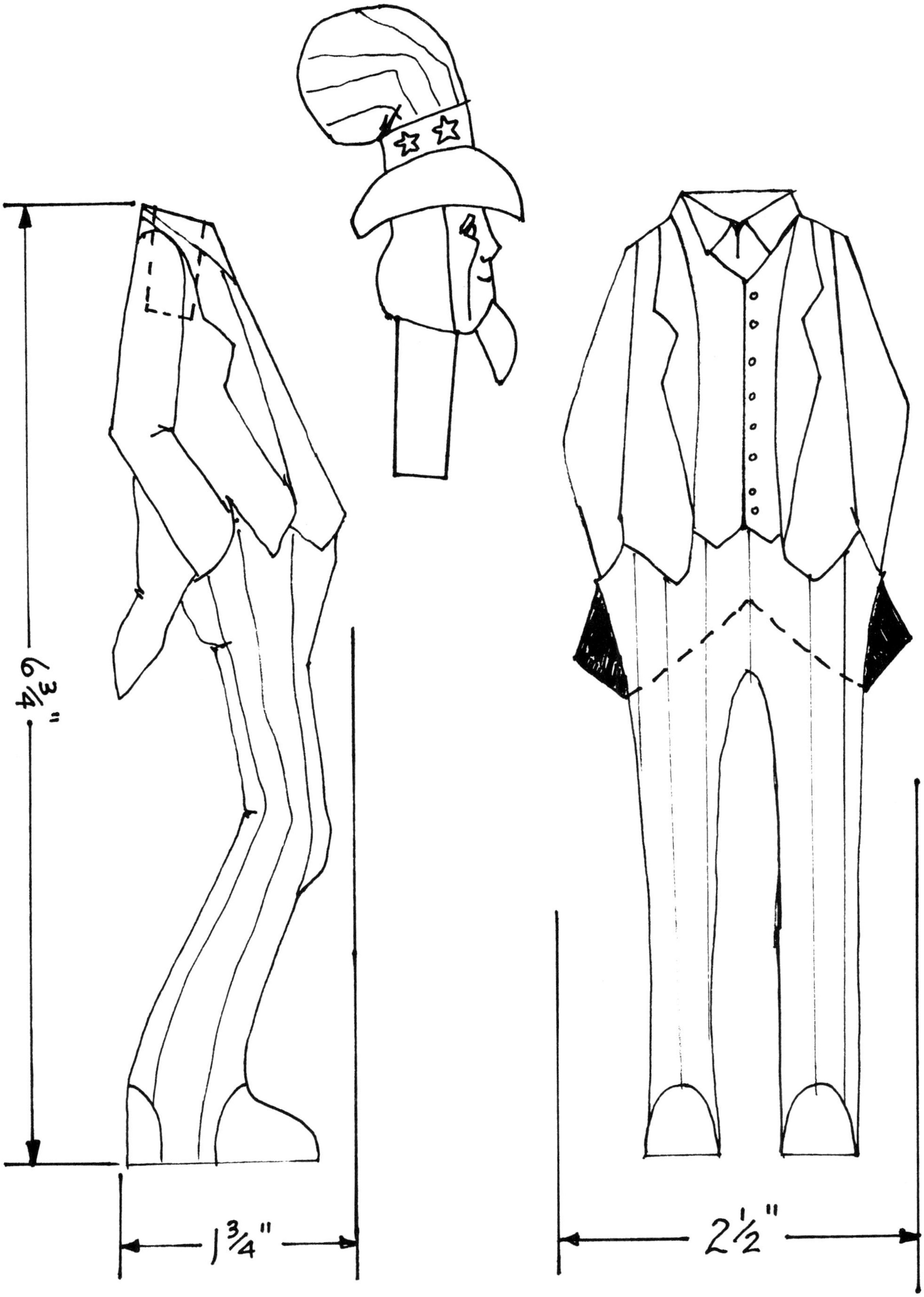

Headin' for California

The hands on this pattern are similar to Hand #1 on the template. Carve the walking stick and clothes bag pole from small twigs. It is easiest if you saw out the top and side hand profiles, drill the necessary hole through the hand for the flag pole, rocket, etc., then finish carving and shaping the hand.

The bag is carved from a piece of scrap wood. Drill a hole through it to slide it on the pole. Adjust the size of the hole in the right hand to fit the walking stick.

Make a base of your choice. Stain or paint it as you desire.

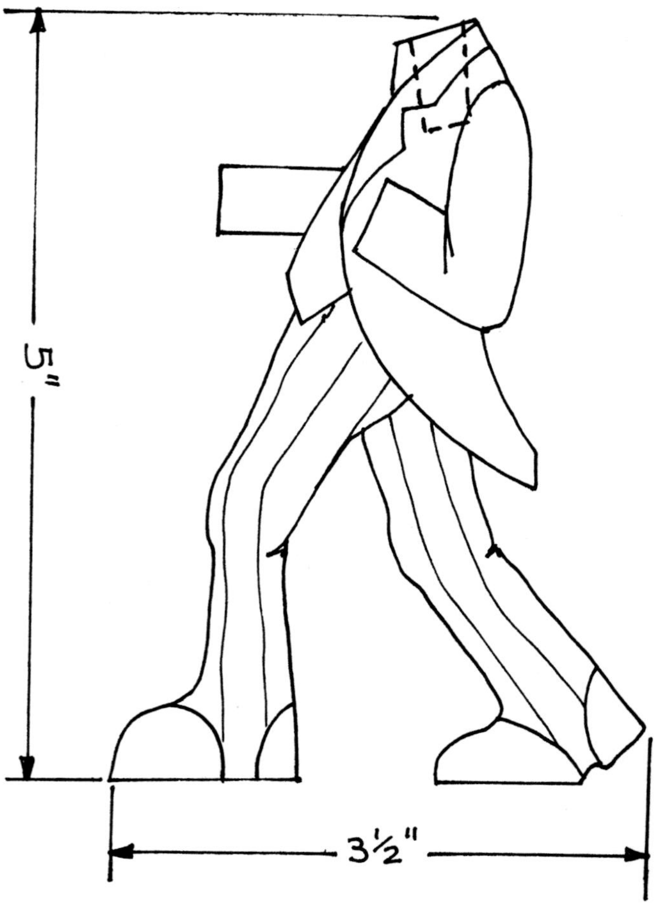

Enlarge 120% for original size.

Whirligig Weathervane

Use a section of 3/4" wood for the main body. Carve both sides the same. Drill a 3/16" hole through the body where the "+" is shown.

Cut the arm from a piece of 3/4" wood. Drill a 3/16" hole through the arm where the "+" is shown. Turn the arm on its side and saw it in half lengthwise. This will give you two arms, each 3/8" thick.

Drill a 1/4" hole in the belly as shown by the dotted lines. Make a base of your choice, large enough to support the weathervane, and drill a 1/4" hole in it. Cut a 1/4" piece of wooden dowel to connect the weathervane to the base. Stain or paint the dowel and base a color of your choice.

Paint the body and arms using the general painting guidelines in the front of the book.

Insert a 3/16" wooden dowel through the body, and cut it so approximately 1/4" protrudes from each side. Put a drop of glue on one dowel end, and slide an arm in place, but do not let it touch the body. Repeat for the other arm, but insure the other arm is pointing in the opposite direction, as shown. When the glue is dry, the arms should spin freely.

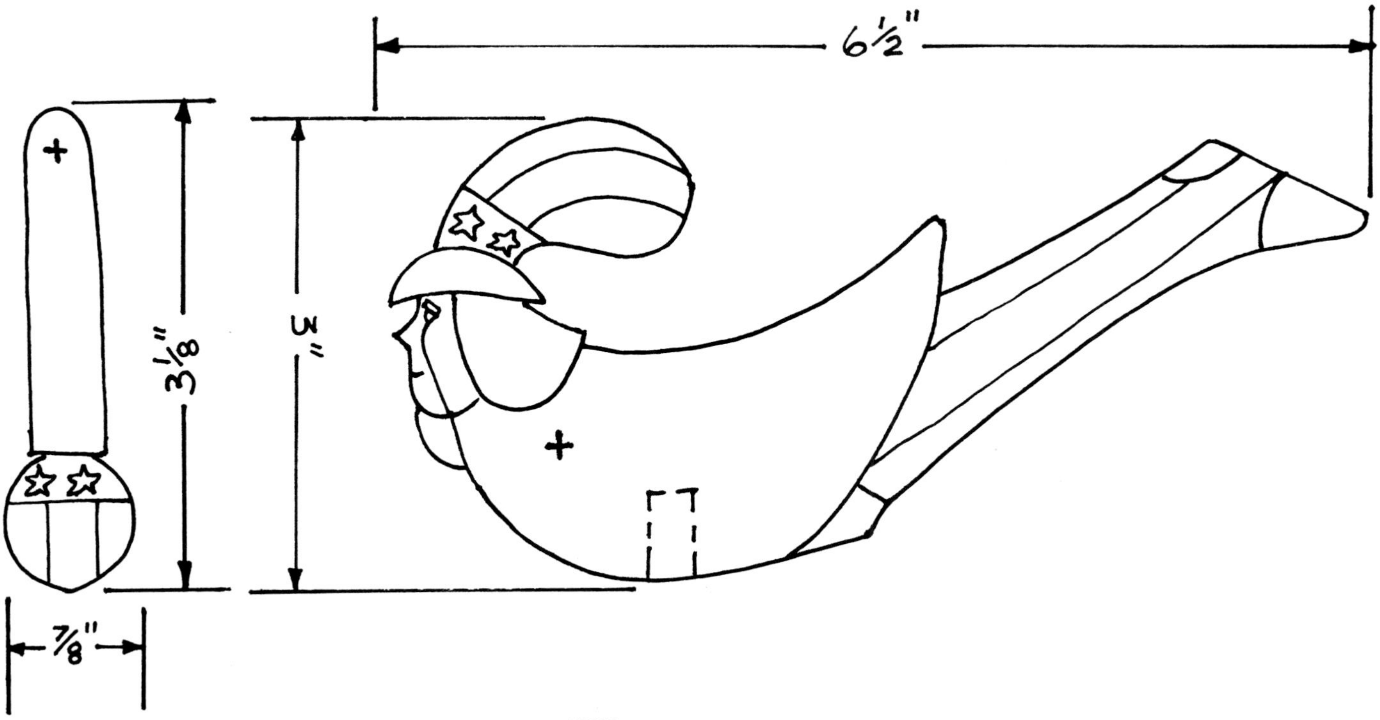

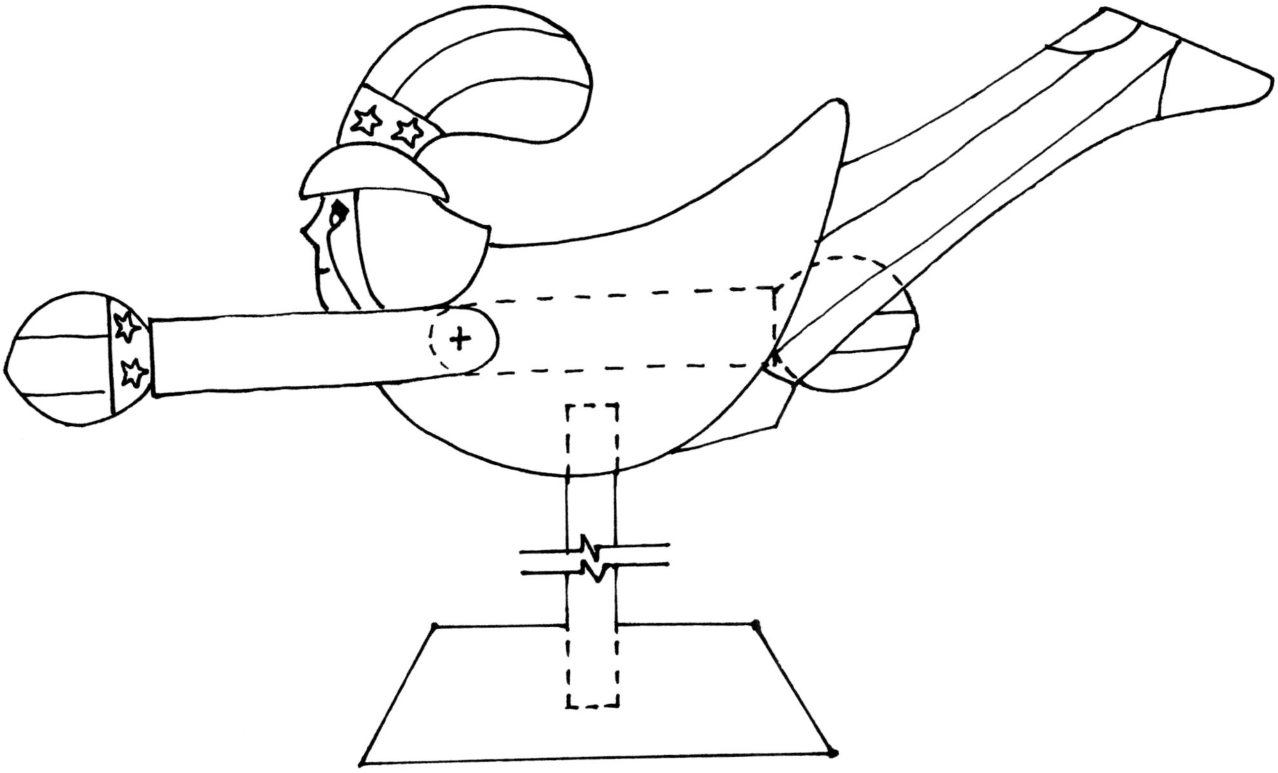

Enlarge 120% for original size.

Christmas Sam

Cut this pattern from a piece of 3/4" thick wood. Carve both sides the same. The bag will only be going over one shoulder, but both arms and hands are holding it.

Drill a 1/4" hole in the belly as shown by the dotted lines. Make a base of your choice, and drill a 1/4" hole in it. Cut a piece of 1/4" wooden dowel to connect the Sam to the base. Stain or paint the dowel and base a color of your choice.

Paint the main body of Sam using the guidelines in the front of the book.

The hat rim is NAVY Blue with White stars. The hat stripes are alternating Napthol Red and White. The ball on the hat tip is White.

The front part of the bag is NAVY Blue with White stars. The back part of the bag is alternating stripes of Napthol Red and White.

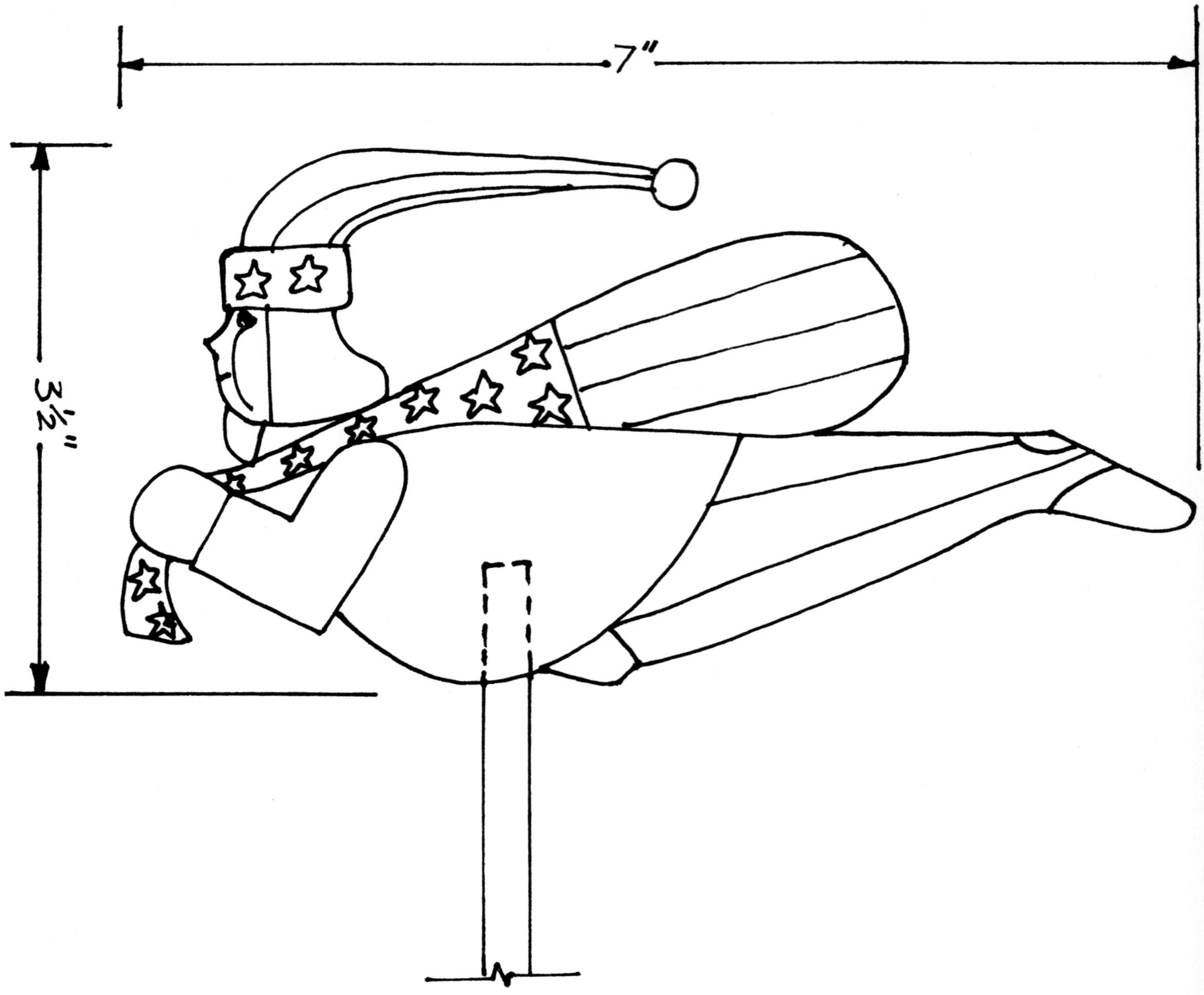

Hand Studies

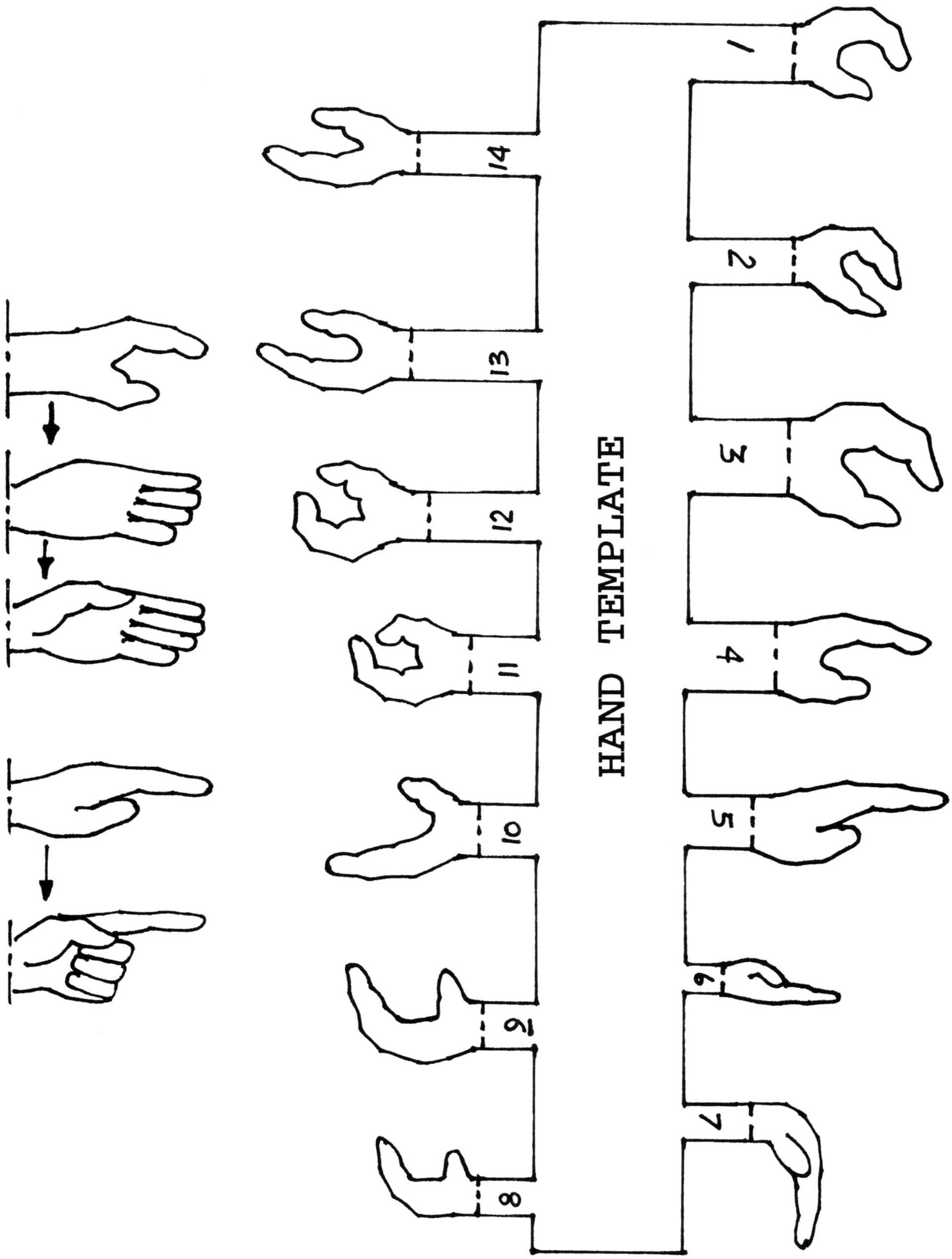

1 5/8"
1 3/8"
6 1/8"

Carving the Head

For this project, we are going to carve one of my versions of an "I Want You" Uncle Sam. We will do it in three phases, much the same way as I do when I am carving figures and caricatures. We will carve the head first. This is the **most** important part of a character carving, because it determines the carving's personality.

The body and hands just complement the head and face. After the head is carved, we will carve the body. Finally, we will carve the hand. This last step will give you a chance to use my "magic" hand template. I will discuss the hand template in more detail during that section of the carving project. If you're ready, let's get started.

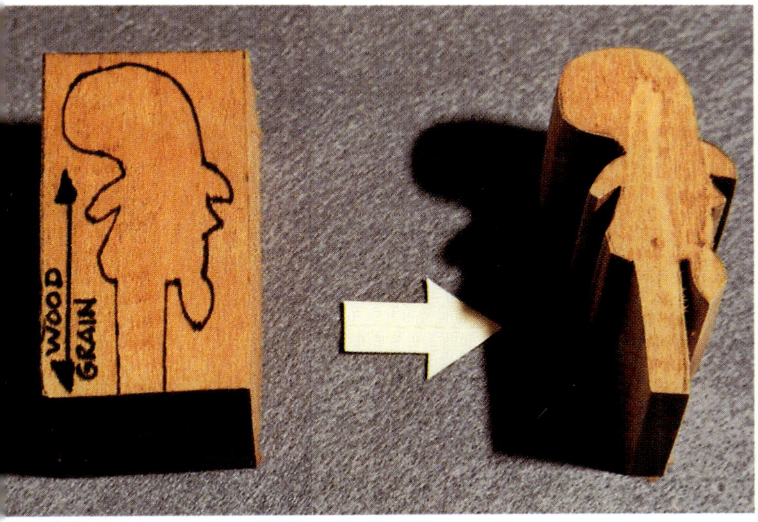

Transfer the head pattern to the wood and saw it out, using a bandsaw, coping saw, or other means. Pay close attention to the direction of the wood grain in the photo. You want the grain to run vertically through the head. This will make carving easier, and will give the head maximum strength.

Sketch in the side view of the hat brim, and the front view of the crown, as shown by the heavy dark lines in the photo. This is an area you can experiment with on future carvings. The width of the crown from left to right will determine the width of the face and hair, as you will see in a later step.

In this front view, you can see where I have darkened the wood I want to remove, in order to establish the rough shape of the crown. **I will use this darkened wood method, when possible, in all future steps of the carving project, to help you see what wood is to be removed.**

Now, clamp the head securely in a vise. Clamp the neck area, so the hat will be clear for you to work on. Using a coping saw, cut in *horizontally* from the sides, along the **top** of the brim, until you reach the vertical lines you drew earlier for the crown width. Next, saw *down* from the top, following the vertical lines, until you connect with the horizontal cuts. The section of wood should fall away, leaving the crown and upper brim roughly shaped and ready for some preliminary carving.

Viewing the head from the top, sketch the **outside** edges of the brim. I prefer a slightly oval shape, from front to back, but you can use a round shape if you prefer.

Starting from the rear center of the **upper** side of the brim, use a small gouge to cut a "U" shaped channel in the brim. The channel should follow the shape of the brim you outlined in the previous step. Don't press too hard or go too deep for now. Work the channel forward until you get about halfway around each side of the crown.

About halfway around, you may have noticed the wood grain starting to "fight" you. At this point, go to the front center of the **upper** side of the brim, and start working toward the rear of the brim, until you have cut a channel all the way around the crown.

Now, remove the head from the vise, and use your knife to remove all the sharp edges from the crown. You want to achieve a fairly rounded shape for the crown, but it doesn't have to be totally smooth. Leaving some of the knife cuts and facets in the wood will give the hat some "character".

Next, draw a line as shown, on the side of the head, to define where the bottom of the hat will rest on the head.

We now want to separate the hat from the head, so we can carve the face and hair **easily**. (This trick also works on cowboys, and any other carvings wearing a hat). Lay the head on its *side* and saw along the line you drew earlier. After separating the two pieces, rub a small amount of wood glue into the **top** of the head, and **bottom** of the hat. This will seal the wood and will make a better joint when we glue the pieces back together later.

With the head facing you, draw two curved reference lines to define the outer edges of the hair. You want the hair to appear to be going into the hat, so these lines will be governed by how wide you made the crown earlier.

Next, lay the head on its *back* and saw away the darkened areas. When you are done, the head and hair will be ready for detailing.

Draw two inner vertical reference lines, to establish the approximate width of the face and neck. Moving these two lines closer together will give you more hair and a narrower face. Moving them apart will give less hair and a fatter face. Experiment with these to give your faces various looks and expressions.

Sketch in the goatee outline. Remove the darkened wood as shown, and round off all the sharp edges of the goatee. Do not carve on the neck yet.

The head and goatee thus far.

Now draw a **vertical** line down the side of the head, as shown. (Do this on both sides of the head, about midway between the front and back of the head). Using the tip of your knife, incise along this line about 1/8" deep. Next, shave in from the front of the head, until the piece of wood comes free. Repeat this until the side depth reaches the *vertical* lines you drew earlier down the *front* of the face.

Draw a horizontal line, as shown,to define the jaw line and the bottom of the hair.

Incise along this line and shave up toward it, from the neck. Repeat this process until the bottom of the hair is well-defined, and the neck is approximately the same width as the face.

Next, use your knife and remove the sharp corners of the face at about a 45 degree angle. This is the first step in the face detailing, and will start the process of rounding out the face.

Remove the new sharp edges that resulted from the last step. Repeat this process until the face is gently rounded from the front, around to the sides.

Sketch in the eye and nose lines as shown in the photo. To make eye sockets, and to create the nose, you will use the tip of your knife and incise the wood about 1/8" deep along the lines you drew. Make the cut a little deeper at the inside corners where the top of the eyes meet the top of the nose.

Starting at the tip of the nose, take your knife and "shave" up toward the eye. Make the cut deeper as you approach the top of the nose. Taking away more and more wood as you reach the top of the nose will make the nose stand out from the cheeks, and will also create eye sockets. Do this procedure for both sides of the nose. Now is the time to drill eye holes and insert the eyes, if you are going to use the quilt pin method I explained in the Tips section.

Let's do a bit more shaping on the nose. Draw a slanted line across the lower corners of the nose. Cut these off with your knife, then round off all the sharp edges.

Now that we have given Uncle Sam some eyes and a nose, let's do some work on the mouth and chin area. Draw some curved lines down from the edges of the nose, to the top of the goatee. Incise these lines with your knife, about 1/8" deep. Now, working from the **center** of the face towards each line you just incised, shave away some wood to form a mouth "mound". There should be *no* wood removed at the very center of the face, and the *most* wood should be shaved away at the edge of each line you incised. (About 1/8" deep).

Sketch a mouth line across the mound you just shaped. Don't quite go all the way across. Now, take your knife or a small "V" gouge and cut a "v" groove on the line. Remove small triangular pieces at the corners of the mouth groove to give it some character.

Next, scoop out a small amount of wood under the lower lip, to help define the chin.

Now, use your knife to remove the sharp edges of the hair at the front and rear of the head. Give all the hair a soft, rounded shape. Experienced carvers may want to use their gouges now to give the hair and goatee more detailing.

Draw a center line down the back of the neck, and continue this line across the bottom of the neck.

Sketch a circle on the bottom of the neck to aid you when we round and shape the neck in the next step.

Using your knife,remove all four sharp edges of the neck. Continue shaving away the sharp edges that arise, until you achieve a fairly rounded neck.

At this point, we are through with the head and face carving. Look it over, and remove any sharp edges that don't appeal to you. When you are satisfied, hold the head against the bottom of the hat, centered under the crown. Trace around the head with a pencil to establish a reference line, then set the head aside temporarily so you can finish carving the hat.

To complete the rough shaping of the hat, use your knife to cut away the darkened sections of the brim, as shown in the photo.

Now, use your knife to **gently** remove the sharp edges from the underside of the hat brim. Be careful not to carve past the reference line. (You need to keep that area flat, so the head will glue flush to the hat).

Place a small amount of wood glue on the top of the head. Press it against the bottom of the hat, in the area you defined with your pencil earlier. Hold the pieces together for about 30 seconds to give the glue time to begin forming a bond.

This completes the head carving. Now, we need to make a body for the head to sit on.

Carving the Body

Transfer the side view of the body pattern to the wood and saw it out, using a bandsaw, coping saw, or other means. Notice that I sawed one piece of wood from the top of the collar around to the top of the arm, and the other piece of wood from the bottom of the toes up to the bottom of the arm. You will also see small "tabs" which I left attached to the rear of the legs, and also to the rear of the coat. These will help hold the body level when I saw out the front view.

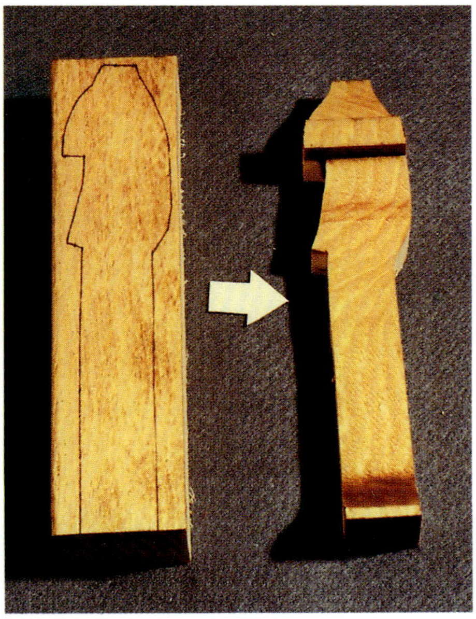

Lay the body on its back, and temporarily replace the two pieces of wood you sawed from the front. You may prefer to use tape to hold the pieces of wood in place while marking and sawing. Transfer the front view of the pattern to the wood, and saw it out. Finally, turn the body on its side, and carefully saw the tabs away.

To make a hole in the collar for the head, take a drill bit that is slightly larger than the neck you carved, and drill a hole straight down into the body as indicated by the dotted lines on the pattern. You may want to clamp the body in a vise while you do this.

Trim the neck as needed, to make a snug fit in the neck hole. Adjust the length so the head rests against the top of the collar.

Sketch in the right arm. Remove the darkened section of wood using your knife or a flat gouge.

Round off the front edges of the coat.

Round off the back edges of the coat, and the back edge of the right arm.

Draw the inside of the right arm.

Mark the back of the right arm. Use your knife or a small "v" gouge to cut a small "v" channel up the back and over the shoulder, until the right arm is well-defined.

Outline the left arm and hand.

Incise these lines about 1/8" deep. Starting from the chest, cut back toward the lines you just incised. Repeat this process of incising and cutting back, until the right arm stands out from the chest.

Trim all the sharp edges off the right arm, and round off the sharp shoulder edges. You will also notice a couple of folds I carved in the elbow area.

Using your knife or "v" gouge, follow the outline all the way around, making a small "v" channel to define the left arm.

As you did for the right arm earlier, trim from the chest, back toward the left arm, until the front part of the arm stands out from the body. Then, trim from the back toward the left arm, until the back part of the arm stands out from the body.

Carve and shape the left hand. Use a knife or small "v" gouge to define the fingers.

Shave back toward these lines until the wood comes free. This will give the coat some definition, and make it stand out from the body. On the sides, you may need to take off a little more wood, so the coat will stand out from the legs.

Round off the sharp edges of the left arm and shoulder. Next, use your knife or small "v" gouge to make a small "v" channel to separate the hand from the sleeve, following the horizontal line you sketched on the arm earlier.

Draw the coat in front, and down around the sides. Incise these lines with your knife about 1/8" deep.

Sketch in the lapels of the coat up the front, and around the back of the collar. Follow these lines using a small "v" gouge.

Remove a small "v" notch in the center of the collar, then sketch in the top of the vest, and the collar tabs.

Now, sketch the bottom of the vest, and the line up the center of the vest. Incise them about 1/8" deep. Shave up toward the vest bottom until the wood comes free. Then, shave toward the left side of the vest, so the left half of the vest stands out slightly more than the right side. Add buttons using a small nailset or eye punch.

Draw a line down the center of the legs and shoes in the front and back. Use a knife or "v" gouge to make a "v" channel about 1/8" deep.

Using your knife, incise these lines about 1/8" deep. Shave down toward the vest top until the wood comes free. Then remove the wood in the collar tab area so the collar tabs and vest top are well-defined.

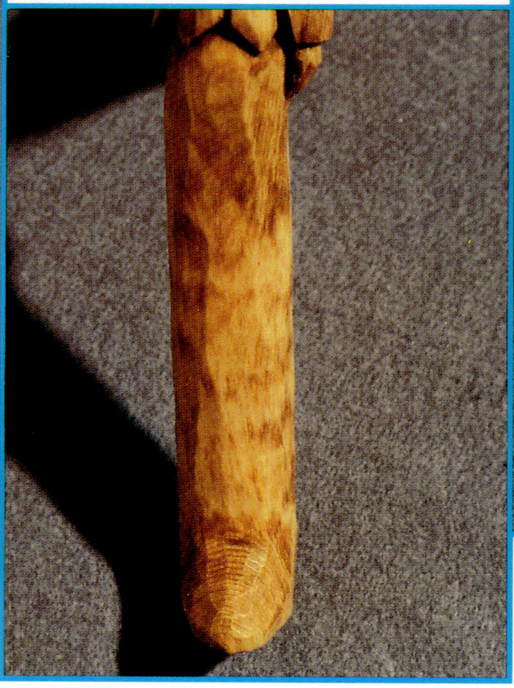

Next, round off the sharp edges of the legs and shoes.

Draw in the lines where the pants go down the side of the shoes. Incise them about 1/8" deep, then shave toward them until the pants stand out from the shoes. This completes the body carving. Look over your carving, and adjust any areas that seem out of balance.

Carving the Hands

Now we'll get to put the hand template to work. Since this is an "I Want You" carving, hands number 5 and 6 on the template are the ones we need to examine. Hold these two against the cuff of the right arm. It looks like hand number 6 is about the right size for this carving, so that's the one we will use.

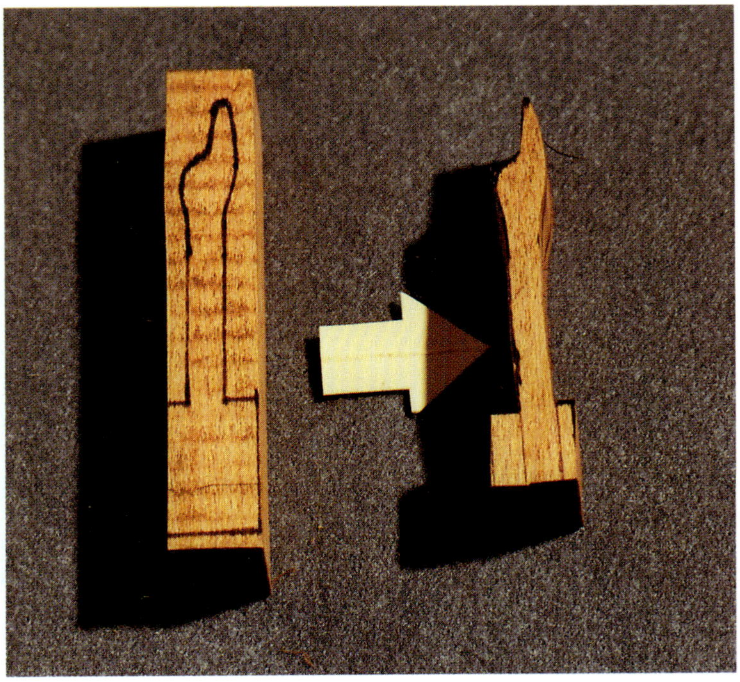

Lay out the top view of the hand on a piece of wood. Notice I have drawn an extended wrist, and left a block at the back to serve as a temporary "handle" while I carve. Saw out the top profile of the hand.

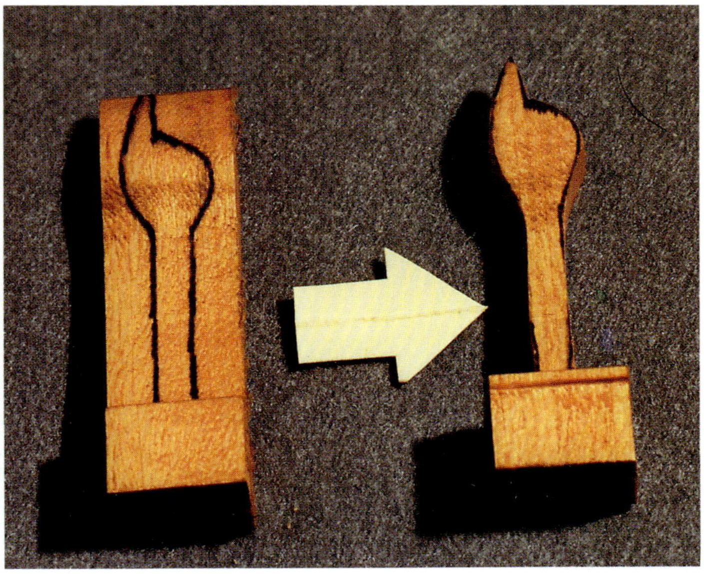

Now, using the bottom set of hands in the Hand Studies as a reference, sketch in the side profile of the hand, then saw it out. You now should have a hand that will require very little work to finish.

Use your knife and round off all the sharp edges of the hand. Next, sketch in the thumb.

Incise around the thumb outline, and shave away about 1/8" of wood so the thumb will stand out from the fingers. Round off the sharp edges of the thumb.

Draw the other three fingers, then use your knife or small "v" gouge to separate and define them. Make sure you continue the separation from the palm side around to the front side of the hand. When carving hands, don't forget your own hands are a valuable reference tool.

Now, cut off the hand squarely, right behind the thumb area. Center and insert a quilt pin about 1/4" deep into the flat end of the right arm, then snip it off, leaving about 1/8" protruding from the arm.

Center the hand, then press it firmly against the arm. Remove the hand, put a drop of glue on the arm, then put the hand back on, using the pin hole in the hand as a reference. Wipe away any excess glue. The pin will hold the hand in place while the glue dries, and will give the joint extra strength. (This also works when gluing heads and hats back together). Once the glue is dry, trim the wrist down if needed, so the hand will appear to be coming out of the coat sleeve. At this point, we have finished carving the project. Now, we'll paint Uncle Sam, put him together, and bring him to life.

Painting the Project

Paint the face and neck with FLESHTONE. Next, put a small amount of SWEETHEART BLUSH on the mouth and cheek areas, then use a dry brush to swirl and blend it into the flesh area. Paint the hands with FLESHTONE, also.

Paint the hair, eyebrows and goatee WHITE. If you used the quilt pin method for eyes, paint them WHITE now. If not, paint a small WHITE line in the crease of the eye socket.

Now take a small, fine-tip brush and put a round dot of BLUE HEAVEN in the center of the eye.

When this is dry, use your fine-tip brush to put a BLACK dot inside the BLUE dot. The placement of the BLUE and BLACK dots will have various effects on Uncle Sam's facial expression. Experiment on a piece of scrap wood to discover all the expressions you can create. I personally like to show the eyes rolled upward, looking toward one side or the other. You may experiment with different looks and find one that you prefer also.

Finally, take a toothpick and put a WHITE highlight on the edge of the BLACK dot. If the eyes are looking to the left, I put the highlight around the 10 o'clock position. If looking to the right, I put the highlight around the 2 o'clock position. When looking straight ahead, as they are here, you can put the highlight at either the 10 o'clock or 2 o'clock position, whichever you prefer. This is another area you can experiment with on a scrap piece of wood, to see the effects of moving the highlight around.

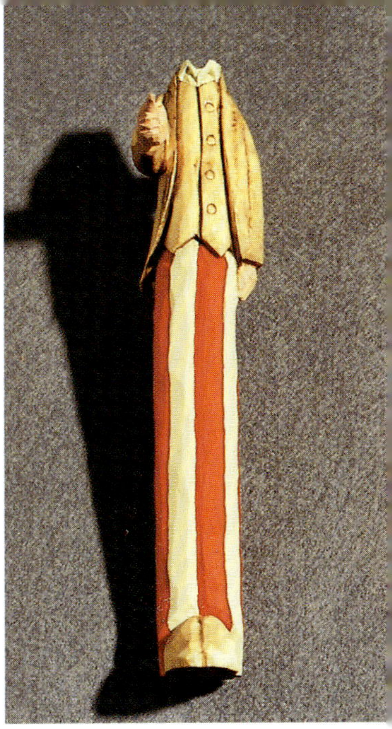

Paint the hat brim and lower part of the crown NAVY BLUE. Divide the upper part of the crown into eight approximately equal sections. Paint these sections alternating colors of NAPTHOL RED and WHITE. Finally, use your stylus and paint small WHITE stars around the lower part of the crown.

Divide the pants legs into eight approximately equal sections. Paint these sections alternating NAPTHOL RED and WHITE as you did the upper part of the hat. Also, paint the shirt collar WHITE.

Paint the vest ANTIQUE GOLD.

Paint the coat NAVY BLUE.

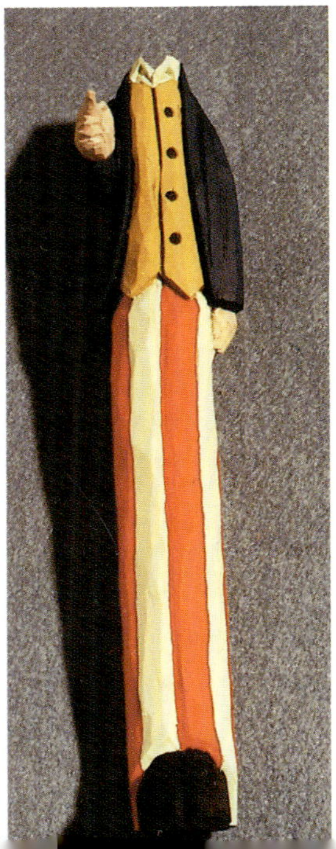

Paint the shoes, and the buttons on the vest BLACK. We are now through with painting Uncle Sam. If you wish to antique your project, I have included some instructions below. I would suggest that you do this before you glue the head to the body.

"Antiquing"

Once the paint is dry, you may want to "age" your Uncle Sam with an antiquing product. I have had excellent results using antiquing gels made by Delta Technical Coatings. These are available at hobby and craft stores. They come in various colors, so you can create different effects.

Brush a coat of antiquing gel on the carving, then wipe it off using a damp rag or sponge. It is your option how much you wipe off. After the antiquing is dry, I like to finish my carvings with a coat of brush-on acrylic varnish. Delta Technical Coatings also makes an excellent varnish. I prefer the one that leaves a Satin finish. This particular finish is not too flat nor too glossy, but leaves a "soft" look to the completed carving. **(I usually put a coat of varnish on the face and hair area BEFORE I antique the carving. This will prevent these areas from absorbing too much antiquing color.)**

When you are ready to assemble your project, put a drop of glue in the neck hole of the body. Insert the head, and position it looking straight ahead, or looking to the side (your option). I believe the carvings have more "life" to them, when the head is looking to the side. I also made a base for my project from a scrap piece of wood, and glued Uncle Sam to it for more stability.

When everything is dry, sign your name, and put the date on the bottom of the carving. After you become a famous carver, your signature will make your carvings more valuable. I also number my carvings, and include this number along with my signature and date. I keep a record book of sequential numbers, along with a brief description of the carving. Many times, collectors will not buy a carving unless it has a signature and a number. As your carvings become more and more "collectible", the lower numbered ones will increase in value to collectors.

Conclusion

Your carvings are a reflection of your talent and skill... be proud of that, and put that signature on there so the whole world will know who made that masterpiece! Take a few minutes now to sit back and admire your creation.

I hope that in some way I have been able to help each of you with some aspect of carving and painting. When we share tips and information, we all become better. If you have any comments or questions about something in this book, or if you have an idea you'd like to see me put in a future book, please feel free to write or call me at the following address and telephone number. I welcome any comments or suggestions you have.

Al Streetman
1609 N. Fordson Drive
Oklahoma City, Ok. 73127
(405) 495-0816

Right side view

Front view

Left side view

The Finished Project

Rear view

The Gallery

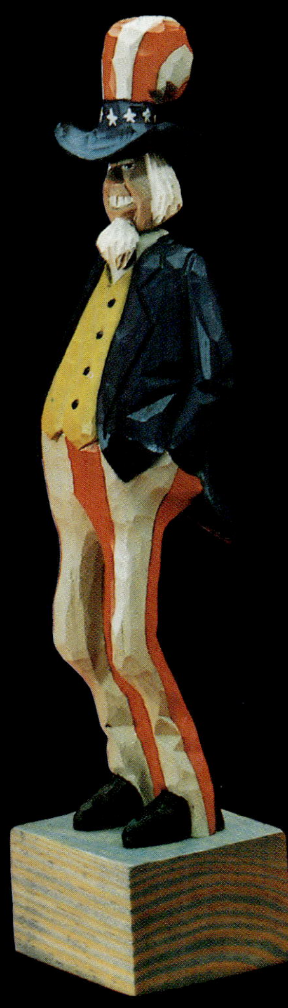

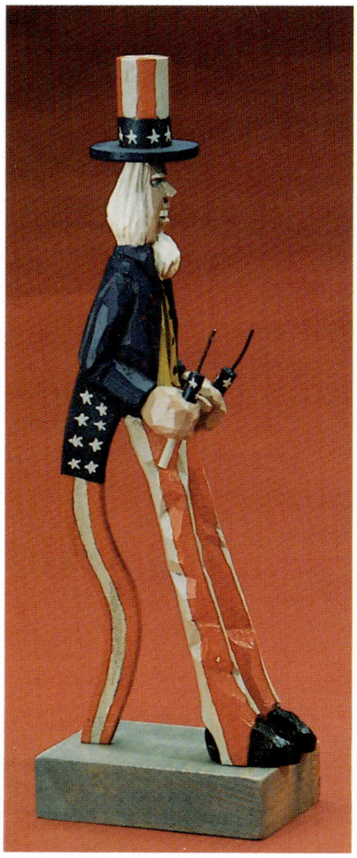